HEADING OUT ON YOUR OWN:

31 Life Skills in 31 Days

Heading Out
ON YOUR OWN:

31 Life Skills in 31 Days

BRETT H. MCKAY AND KATE R. MCKAY

First Printing, 2013

ISBN 978-0-9891903-9-8

Semper Virilis Publishing
PO Box 978
Jenks, OK 74037

www.sempervirilis.com

Cover Design by Eric Granata
Illustrations by Ted Slampyak
Photography by Daren Bush, Antonio Centeno,
            Brett McKay, and Matt Moore
Typesetting and graphics by erikka hedberg DESIGN

CONTENTS

INTRODUCTION

1

DAY 1:

Develop a Self-Reliant Mentality

7

DAY 2:

How to do Laundry

17

DAY 3:

How to Open and Manage a Checking Account

33

DAY 4:

Keep a Regular Grooming and Hygiene Routine

47

DAY 5:

Create a Weekly Attack Plan

57

DAY 6:

How to Ace a Job Interview

71

DAY 7:

How to Make a Bed

83

DAY 8:

Living With Roommates

87

DAY 9:

Managing Your Online Reputation

99

DAY 10:

How to Tie the Half-Windsor Necktie Knot

121

DAY 11:

Understand Credit

125

DAY 12:

What to Do If You Get in a Car Accident

137

DAY 13:

Know How to Network

149

DAY 14:

Establish a Simple Cleaning Routine and Stick to It

165

DAY 15:

How to Change a Flat Tire

171

DAY 16:

Create a Budget

175

DAY 17:

Essential Etiquette for Young Men

189

DAY 18:

Renting Your First Apartment

201

DAY 19:

Fix a Running Toilet

219

DAY 20:

Maintaining Your Car

231

DAY 21:

Know Your Way Around a Kitchen

243

DAY 22:

How to Make Small Talk

273

DAY 23:

How to Iron a Dress Shirt

293

DAY 24:

How to Be a Savvy Consumer

297

DAY 25:

Establish an Exercise Routine

311

DAY 26:

15 Maxims for Being a Reliable Man

323

DAY 27:

How to Shop for Groceries

339

DAY 28:

How to Jump Start a Car

355

DAY 29:

How to Iron Your Trousers

359

DAY 30:

How to Manage Stress

375

DAY 31:

A Place for Everything & Everything in Its Place

395

CONCLUSION

419

INTRODUCTION

Growing up, Dwight D. Eisenhower was responsible for many chores around the house and for looking after his younger brothers. When his mother got sick and was quarantined in a room in the house for several months, Ike was responsible for cooking for his whole family — his mother would call directions to him from her bed on how to make the meals (an experience that gave Ike a lifelong love of cooking). When Eisenhower graduated from high school, he started working as an engineer in a creamery's ice plant. He worked 84 hours a week on the night shift — from 6pm to 6am, 7 days a week, 52 weeks a year. Even with his savings, he didn't want his college education to put any burden on his parents, so he decided to apply to the Naval Academy. He and a friend sent away for past entrance examinations, and after working all night, Ike would sleep a few hours and then go over to the gas lighting store where his friend was employed, and together they would study every afternoon before Ike had to be back at the ice plant. Eisenhower ended up at West Point and was able to hit the ground running when he got there. That was 1915.

In 2001, I, Brett McKay, graduated from high school and after a summer working at a paint shop, left home to become a freshman at the University of Oklahoma. I had never done my own laundry. I had never cleaned my own bathroom. I had never cooked for myself (unless plates of nachos count). I was a typical middle-class kid from the burbs, and the first time I moved away from home, I floundered. I finished the fall semester with a 2.6 GPA, and moved back home to go to a local college in my hometown. I just didn't know how to live on my own successfully.

My parents, God bless 'em, had tried to prepare me for leaving the nest, but they were also willing to do a lot of things for me, and as a teenager lacking foresight, I didn't see a reason to look the gift horse in the mouth and learn how to do them myself. I eventually learned a lot of the basic life skills I had once been lacking, but I wish I had prepared myself a little better to become independent and self-reliant once I had flown the coop. Every fall, millions of young men around the country get ready to head off to college and/or move out on their own. In an effort to help these young men avoid the same hapless mistakes I made, and better navigate the waters of independence, we decided to put together this book.

The goal is simple: **to help young men heading out on their own for the first time learn some of the very basic life skills they'll need to succeed once they're living on their own.** If that's you, think of this book as a 31-day boot camp on becoming a successful, well-adjusted adult. If you've already been living on your own for a short time, or even for decades, but either never got around to learning some of these life skills, or simply need to brush up on them, this book is for you, too.

We've divided it into 31 chapters or "days." Each day, you'll learn a different basic life skill that will help you become self-sufficient as you head out on your own for the first time. We cover everything from shopping for groceries and stocking your kitchen, to ironing your clothes, to properly dealing with stress, and many more of the things that get taken for granted or just don't apply when living at home. When possible, try to perform, practice, or implement the skill on the day that it's covered. At the same time, keep in mind that some of these skills will require more than a few hours to master; the traits having to do with your mindset, in particular, will be things you'll work on over a lifetime. No matter the type of skill, you'll make mistakes and fail along the way. Don't get discouraged – just keep working on them. If it makes you feel any better, I've been living on my own for over ten years, and I'm still working on some of these "basic" life skills!

Alright, you'll be packing your bags and heading out the door before you know it, so let's get cracking on transforming you from dependent boy to self-sufficient man.

DAY 1

Develop a
Self-Reliant
Mentality

———◆———

This first task is really more of a mindset than a skill set, but it's a crucial building block that will lay the foundation for the rest of the "harder," more practical skills we'll be covering in this book.

It's developing a self-reliant mentality.

Part of being a grown man is taking care of yourself and making your own decisions. It isn't until you're on your own that you realize how much you relied on adults to make your life run smoothly. From doing your laundry to calling the doctor when you were sick, your parents likely did a lot of things for you.

While you might not be completely self-sufficient right when you move out (many young people rely on their parents for varying degrees of financial support well into their twenties), you can certainly be self-reliant in a number of areas in your life. For example, you shouldn't need your mom to remind you about important appointments or your dad to bug you about taking your car in to get its routine maintenance. You should be able to remember to do those things yourself. A man with a self-reliant mentality doesn't wait around for someone else to take care of things that need to be taken care of. If he encounters a problem, he takes the initiative and tries to figure out how to resolve it himself.

So how does a man develop a self-reliant mentality?

One of the best answers I have found to this question actually comes from a great, albeit endearingly cheesy, 1950s educational film called "Developing Self-Reliance." It's ten minutes long and definitely worth watching (*http://youtu.be/xGROmq1mX1o*).

In the film, a kind-hearted teacher lays out the four principles of building self-reliance for one of his young students:

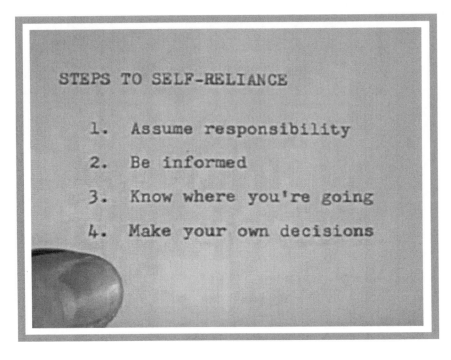

STEPS TO SELF-RELIANCE

1. Assume responsibility
2. Be informed
3. Know where you're going
4. Make your own decisions

1. Assume responsibility. Start taking responsibility for your life and the things in it. If you've relied on your mom to wake you up every morning so you weren't late to school, it's time to make friends with the alarm clock on your smartphone. Start using a calendar to keep track of your appointments and important due dates. When you notice your apartment or dorm room is looking messy, clean it up. Don't blame your teacher or your boss if you're not doing well in a class or at work. If you make a mistake, own up to it, and try to make it right yourself instead of immediately running back to mom and dad so they can fix it for you. When you come home to visit your parents, don't fall back into old routines and let mom do your laundry for you. Parents sacrifice much in taking on not only their own burdens, but the burden of responsibility for each of their children as well. But they should not have to carry more than their own burdens indefinitely; when a child is able, he, in gratitude to the unselfish care he received for many years from his parents, should begin to transfer his load from their shoulders to his, as soon as he possibly can.

I'll be honest with you. Taking responsibility for your life isn't all that fun. It requires doing things that are often boring, tedious, frustrating, and time-consuming. You'll feel the burden of weighing a hard decision and accepting the consequences, even if they're not favorable to you. You'll often go un-praised and un-rewarded for being responsible.

But taking responsibility for your life *is* satisfying. You'll gain a quiet confidence in yourself as you take control of your own life. You'll feel empowered. Instead of feeling like life is simply happening to you, you'll begin to feel like the captain of your destiny and master of your soul. As you assume responsibility for your life, you'll notice doors open up to new and better opportunities. While you may notice that other young men who don't take responsibility for their lives seem to enjoy a life of worry-free ease, give it a few years: those same men will probably have progressed little and seem stuck in neutral. You can have little responsibility, a ton of fun and pleasure, and few life options, or a healthy amount of responsibility, a healthy amount of fun and pleasure, and a ton of life options. I personally endorse the latter option. As the vintage film on self-reliance puts it, while it's easy to get by having other people do everything for you, "the trouble is, when you're not self-reliant, you'll never do more than just get by."

2. Be informed. Of course in order to take on more responsibilities, you have to know how to carry out those responsibilities. Some young men continue letting mom and dad do things for them, with the excuse that they just don't know how to do those things themselves. They often turn to their parents to make decisions for them for the same reason. But the truth is, they've never actually tried to figure things out on their own.

This excuse is especially weak in the age of the internet, with answers to many of life's practical questions just a Google search away. Need to figure out how to apply for financial aid? Don't pawn the job off on mom — get on the computer and start researching it yourself.

This isn't to say that you should completely avoid mom and dad or other adults for advice and counsel. There are some problems or decisions Google just can't help with. You should definitely take advantage of the practical wisdom older people have acquired by asking for their input when making an important decision or trying to solve a problem.

However, I'd encourage you not to always make your parents a resource of first resort. We frequently turn to our parents when we don't really want input — we want to be told what to do. And when parents hear about your problem, they often want to take care of it for you, even when you protest. So investigate yourself first; try figuring things out on your own. Experience can be the best teacher. Once you've reached a wall, then go talk to your parents. Because you've gotten your hands dirty with your issue, so to speak, you'll be in a better position to ask them effective questions. Instead of feeling like a kid, you'll feel more like a fellow traveler in the land of adulthood who's simply looking for advice from someone who has already been there.

In situations where the stakes are high, turn to others sooner rather than later; oftentimes it's better to learn from the mistakes of others, rather than making them yourself. But by always taking at least the first steps of intelligence gathering yourself whenever you can, you'll grow and make discoveries you wouldn't have otherwise.

The self-reliant man is always looking for a chance to learn and expand his knowledge and skills. He reads books for his classes not because he has to, but because he wants to. And whether he's in college or on the job, he also reads regularly for pleasure. He keeps up with the news and current events. He talks to others and really listens to them. He's very observant wherever he goes. In this way, he builds up a library of information that he can draw upon when making a decision or solving a problem.

3. Know where you're going. A self-reliant man has goals that he has set for himself. His aims are not merely those things other people think he should do. The self-reliant man is autonomous and doesn't overly rely on others to validate his decisions. A self-reliant man works with an end in mind. He has created a blueprint for his future. When he runs into a problem, he informs himself on what an ideal resolution would be and then works to make it a reality. He plans out his weeks and ensures tasks that he's responsible for are completed.

4. Make your own decisions. One thing I've learned the hard way is that life is actually much easier and a lot less stressful when you proactively make your own decisions. It's tempting when you're younger to simply let life happen to you and hope that decisions and problems will magically resolve themselves. They won't. In fact, problems and decisions often get bigger and harrier the longer you wait to take action on them. Make proactive decision-making a habit. With any choice or problem you may face, decide on an action plan quickly, and execute it immediately.

"In any moment of decision, the best thing you can do is the right thing, the next best thing is the wrong thing, and the worst thing you can do is nothing."

–Theodore Roosevelt

Also, while you should certainly seek advice from others to inform your decisions, don't rely on them to make your decisions for you. It's your life. Don't let others live it for you.

BALANCING SELF-RELIANCE

Learning to be self-reliant takes time; you're not magically transformed into a sage, totally autonomous adult the moment you turn 18. Rather, self-reliance is something you develop in stages as you get older, learn from experience, and become more and more independent.

I often get questions like, "When my parents come and visit, is it okay for them to buy me groceries?" "Is it okay for them to pay for my rent?" These men want to know where a young man should draw the line in being self-reliant and receiving assistance from their parents. Unfortunately, I don't have any easy answers for such queries, and I don't think there are any hard and fast rules, either. I would recommend asking yourself this question: "Will this support lead to more independence down the road or will it lead to greater dependence?" For example, a recent study showed that college students who get less financial support from their parents think of themselves as adults sooner, drink less, and may be more career-oriented, while those whose parents give them a free ride are more likely to engage in risky behaviors like binge drinking, and may be less motivated in their studies. On the other hand, students with parents who provide no assistance are more likely to take longer to graduate and drop out altogether. Basically, what the study found was that either too much self-reliance or too little can lead to a compromised college career, and less independence in the future; thus, the authors of that study recommended a balanced approach in which parents provide some assistance, while the student is responsible for other expenses. All of which is to say, it's best to grow into self-reliance in stages — concentrate on becoming self-reliant in whatever you can, wherever you're at in life, in ways that don't compromise your ability to gain more independence in later stages.

DAY 2

How to do
Laundry

———◆———

One of the first things many young men will be confronted with doing for themselves for the first time when they leave home is their laundry. It's not exactly rocket science (none of these 31 basic life skills will be, so let's retire that caveat today), but there is a surprising amount to it — believe it or not, whole books have been written on the subject! Today we'll cover the essentials in an easy-to-follow question and answer format. It's an important skill to learn not just because everybody has to do it every single week without fail, but when you know how to do it properly, you won't ruin your clothes or wear them out too quickly — something a young man on a budget can ill-afford to do. So let's get started.

BEFORE YOU WASH YOUR CLOTHES

HOW OFTEN DO I NEED TO WASH THINGS?

You don't have to wash everything you own after only one use. The less you wash your clothes, the longer they'll last. While a lot depends on how often you shower, how smelly/sweaty you are, how long you wear the garment, the weather, etc., you can generally gauge whether something needs washing by how it feels and smells. Here's a breakdown of how often, on average, to wash your various garments:

Undershirts/underwear/socks — 1 wear. So have plenty of pairs. Don't turn your underwear inside-out for another use! But if you run out, and don't have time for a wash, wash a pair in the sink at night and let it dry for the morning.

T-shirts — 1 wear. They absorb a lot of oil and sweat.

Jeans — every 4-6 wears. Yes, it is possible to go many months without washing your denim (a must, actually, if it's selvedge denim), and if they don't smell, go right ahead; they won't accumulate any more bacteria after 300 wears than 15. You can spot-clean any stains you get (this goes for other clothing too).

Khaki/cargo shorts and pants — every 2-4 wears. Khakis don't hide dirt as well as jeans and absorb more bodily sweat and oil.

Button-down shirts and sweaters — 1-3 wears. Very dependent on how tightly the garment fits to the body, the weather, and how long you wore it. When you take it off, give the armpits a sniff. If they don't smell, put the shirt back on the hanger or drape the sweater over a chair to air out. If it's right on the border, try a shot of Febreze.

Pajamas — 2-3 wears. Depending on how much you sweat at night (although everybody sweats more while sleeping than they realize — around a liter a night).

Towels — once a week. Assuming daily use.

Bed sheets — every two weeks. Experts say to wash bed sheets every week, but I know most young men aren't going to do that. But at least wash them every couple of weeks (if you can't even manage that, at least wash your pillowcase

— especially if you have acne-prone skin). If you need motivation, think of lying around in skin cells, dust mites and their feces, fungal mold and spores, bodily secretions, and bacteria. Not to mention insect parts, pollen, and soil. Sweet dreams.

How Do I Know How to Wash Something?

READ THE LABEL. If you get anything from this chapter, let it be this. **Read the darn label.** It will tell you exactly how to wash, dry, and iron your clothes. Don't worry, you don't need to know the meaning of those crazy laundry symbols you may have seen on your dad's 1980s polo shirt. Clothing manufacturers used to rely on them to tell consumers how to wash a piece of clothing. Today, most clothing companies forego the symbols and literally spell out how you're supposed to wash their clothes. For example, my polo shirt from Criquet Shirts has the following washing instructions: "Machine wash cold. Wash with like colors. Non-chlorine bleach only. Tumble dry low. Warm iron as needed." I checked my other shirts, and all the labels were similar: instructions all spelled out and no symbols.

If a piece of clothing says "Dry Clean Only," then take it to the cleaners. Yes, there are ways you can launder dry-clean-only fabrics at home, but for a beginner it's not worth the risk, and for a young man, probably not worth the hassle. (If you're a low-maintenance guy who's never going to want to get something dry-cleaned, be sure to check the label before you buy something.)

How Do I Sort My Clothing Into Loads?

There are all kinds of elaborate laundry sorting systems out there, but for most young, college-aged men they're overkill.

Here's the system I used during my bachelor years:

First, sort your dirty laundry by color. Many experts recommend creating three different color piles: whites, lights, and darks. In my experience, you just need two: whites and colors. Sorting by color ensures that your white dress shirts don't turn pink from the bleeding crimson from your OU Sooners t-shirt (don't ask).

After sorting by color, sort each pile by fabric heft: lighter fabrics (like dress shirts) in one pile and heavier fabrics (like jeans and sweatshirts) in another pile. I also create a pile that consists of bed linens and towels. Sorting by fabric type becomes important when we dry our laundry. Lighter items, like your t-shirts, dry much more quickly than your heavier items, like towels. When you dry light fabrics with other light fabrics, you can reduce the amount of time the dry cycle takes, which saves you money. This doesn't necessarily mean you'll need to do more loads either; heavier items, like jeans and sweatshirts, don't need to be washed as often as other stuff, so just "save up" until you have one big heavy-item load to do.

WHAT DO I DO ABOUT STAINS?

While the nitty-gritty of stain removal is not within the purview of this chapter, many stains will come out in the wash if you simply pre-treat them with something like Shout. So when you sort through your clothes, be on the lookout for stains.

If you have white dress shirts or light-colored t-shirts in your dirty laundry, make sure to pre-treat your collar and your armpits with stain remover. You don't want that dreaded ring around your collar or yellow armpit stains.

WASHING YOUR CLOTHES

WHAT WATER TEMPERATURE SHOULD I USE?

This can get confusing, but keep it simple: Use warm water for whites; cold water for colors. Now admittedly I used to be a hot water for whites guy, but after researching the heck out of this chapter, I found that most experts agree that with the efficiency of washers and detergents these days, using only warm, or even cold water for all washes is A-okay. You might still want to wash your linens, towels, and gym clothes (regardless of their color) in hot water though, since hot water is best at getting out the grime. But always use cold water for colors, as it fades the color of clothes less than hot water does.

WHAT CYCLE SHOULD I CHOOSE?

Your default cycle should be "regular." It's the longest cycle and has the fastest and most vigorous wash and spin cycles (spin cycles are when the machine spins out the water from the clothes). It's good for all fabric types.

Unless you have the same underclothing tastes as J. Edgar Hoover, you won't use the delicate cycle very often, except for things like sweaters or a nice dress shirt. Remember: **read the label.**

What about the ever-mysterious permanent press cycle? This cycle is for synthetic fabrics like rayon, polyester, and acetate, as well as natural fabrics that have been treated with a chemical to resist wrinkles (like your "no-iron" dress shirts).

The permanent press cycle has a fast wash cycle and a slow spin cycle. The slow spin cycle keeps some of the water in the clothes, which helps prevent wrinkling. The only clothing I can imagine a young man having in his wardrobe that would require permanent press would maybe be a rayon vintage bowling shirt. Other than that, I think you're safe to use the regular cycle for the vast majority of your washing needs.

WHAT LOAD SIZE SHOULD I CHOOSE?

Sometimes you have a crapload of clothes to clean, and other times you may have just a few items. Different amounts of water are required for each situation. The usual load option sizes are small, medium, large, and extra-large.

A typical top-loading machine uses the following scale for judging load size:

- Small: clothing fills 1/3 of wash drum before adding water
- Medium: clothing fills 1/3 to 1/2 of wash drum before adding water
- Large: clothing fills 1/2 to 3/4 of wash drum before adding water
- Extra-large: clothing fills wash drum 3/4 to completely full before adding water

WHAT KIND OF DETERGENT SHOULD I USE? POWDER, LIQUID, HIGH EFFICIENCY (HE)?

Consumerism, for better or for worse, has given us dozens of different kinds of laundry detergents to choose from. So many, in fact, that it can be overwhelming to pick which one to use. While all of them will clean your clothes, each detergent type has pros and cons.

- Powder detergents — cheaper per load than liquid detergents and better at getting out stains like dirt and clay than their liquid cousins. Unless specially formulated, powder detergents don't readily dissolve in cold water like liquid ones.
- Liquid detergents — more expensive, but better at getting out organic stains like blood, grass, and pizza sauce. They also dissolve better in cold water.
- HE detergents — more expensive than regular detergents because they are specifically designed for High Efficiency washers. They are low-sudsing and quick-dispersing for use in low water volume machines. If you're living in the dorms or in apartments with shared laundry facilities, you likely won't have HE washing machines. While you can use HE detergent in regular washing machines, it would be a waste of money to do so.

Detergent companies are now marketing small pods that contain both liquid and powder detergent and dissolve in the wash. While certainly convenient, they're expensive. For a young man on a budget, this probably isn't a good option. Go with the powder.

Here's another money-saving tip about laundry detergent. Experts say you can get away with **using anywhere from 1/2 to 1/8 what the manufacturer recommends** and still come away with clean clothes. I aim for about half the recommended fill line myself.

In addition to choosing between liquid, powder, and pods, you can select scented or unscented detergents. If you're prone to allergies, go with the unscented version.

Finally, fill the washing machine with water and add detergent *before* you add your clothes. While the machine is filling with water, add your detergent. By filling your washing machine with water and detergent before you add your clothes, you ensure that your detergent is evenly distributed throughout the water. Also, pouring detergent right on your clothing can leave spots; this is especially a concern with powder detergents.

SHOULD I USE BLEACH?

Bleaching, if done improperly, will ruin your clothing. But in the hands of a knowledgeable person, bleach can remove stains, make whites whiter, and disinfect the nasty bedsheets you've been lying in all week with the flu. But if you're not comfortable with using bleach, you can honestly get away with skipping it. I didn't use it all that often when I was on my own and my clothes looked fine. Kate's never used it in her life. But if you decide to use it, here are some guidelines.

There are two types of bleaches: chlorine and non-chlorine. Chlorine bleach is the strongest, but it's not safe for all fabrics. It's the bleach that can leave your classic, green polo looking like a groovy tie-dyed shirt if you get some splashed on it.

Non-chlorine bleach, like OxiClean, is safe for colored clothing made with colorfast dyes and fabrics and will make colored clothing look brighter. Non-chlorine bleach, however, isn't as effective as the chlorine variety at brightening whites.

If you decide to use chlorine bleach on your whites or bed linens, pour the instructed amount in the bleach dispenser in the washing machine before starting the cycle. If your machine doesn't have a liquid bleach dispenser, mix the bleach with 1 to 1.5 quarts of water and add it after your clothes have been washing for five minutes. Stir it in with a wooden stick or spoon.

Never pour bleach directly on clothing, even whites. I had to learn this from experience. I poured some bleach on a load of white laundry while the machine was still filling with water. After drying, my white clothes had a bunch of brown stains which I later learned were chemical burns from the bleach. Lesson: use bleach with caution.

WASHING TIPS

Load your clothing a few pieces at a time. With the machine filled with water and your detergent added, you're now ready to add clothing. Don't throw giant, wadded up armfuls of laundry into the machine. Add your clothing a few pieces at a time. This will ensure that all parts of the fabric get adequate agitation in the machine.

Don't cram all your clothing into a single load. In an effort to save time and money, you will be tempted to cram as much of your dirty laundry into a single wash load as possible. Resist that temptation. Your clothes need room in the drum to swish around in order to get clean. If you want clean clothes, don't overload the washing machine.

Close the lid and set a timer. To get the machine to start washing, simply close the lid. Because it's easy to forget you have a load of laundry in the wash, set a timer on your phone (even non-smartphones have a timer!) to remind yourself to check the wash when the machine says it should be done. Nobody likes that rank smell that develops from leaving wet clothes in an empty washing machine for too long (although a toss in a hot cycle on the dryer can often zap the smell if that happens to you).

DRYING YOUR CLOTHES

Not everything goes in the dryer. Remember: **read the label.** Some garments will say things like, "Lay flat to dry." In that case, spread it out flat on a towel, smoothing out the wrinkles. If it doesn't go in the dryer, but doesn't need to be laid flat, you can drape it over a drying rack or a chair. Even if a garment can technically go in the dryer, if you don't want it to shrink — perhaps it was just the right size when you bought it or the freshman fifteen is making your jeans feel tight — go ahead and put it on the drying rack instead of the dryer. And of course, if you're living in a house or apartment that allows line-drying, that's a great option too: no shrinkage, less wear and tear on your clothes, no energy or money used, and that fresh air smell.

Clean out the lint screen. Before you put your wet clothes in the dryer, check the lint screen. A clean lint screen ensures that damp air leaves the machine and your clothes get dry. You may have to clean out the screen in the middle of a large load filled with items prone to shedding fuzzy stuff, i.e., towels, denim, etc. Oh, and make sure to save that lint! It's a fantastic fire-starter.

Place clothing in the dryer a few pieces at a time. Clothes tend to get lumped and knotted together in the wash. Throwing your wet clothes into the dryer in a giant ball will result in some clothes getting super dry and others remaining damp. To avoid this, grab a few items at a time from the washing machine, shake 'em out if they're tangled up, and then place them in the dryer.

Don't cram the dryer. Just as you don't want to cram all your clothes into a single wash cycle, you won't want to cram all your clothes into a single drying cycle. Clothes need space in the dryer to tumble and get completely dry. You'll save yourself time and money in the long run by breaking up your drying into smaller loads.

Throw in a fabric softener sheet. To avoid static cling and to give your clothes that soft, comforting feeling, throw in a fabric softener sheet. For smaller loads, you can use just half a sheet. On many newer washing machines, you have the option to put in liquid fabric softener along with the detergent.

Select the correct drying temperature. Rule of thumb when it comes to drying temperatures: the hotter the drying temperature, the greater the likelihood of shrinking. If the care label on your garment says "Tumble Dry," you can use the "regular" temp setting on your dryer. Regular is the hottest temperature and is suitable for sturdy cottons like towels, t-shirts, underwear, jeans, and sheets.

The "medium" setting is suitable for permanent press clothing — synthetics and fabrics treated with wrinkle-free chemicals.

The "low" setting is for stuff like knits and lingerie. Again, if you're a man, you'll likely have very little clothing that requires this setting.

Remove dried clothes immediately. To avoid wrinkles, remove your dry clothes from the dryer and fold and iron them immediately (we'll be covering these skills later in the book). The longer you let them sit there, the more the wrinkles set.

LAUNDROMAT PROTOCOL

Many young men reading this will likely be washing their clothes in public laundromats and dormitory basements. Washing your clothes in shared machines requires pluck, craftiness, and social grace that you don't need when washing your clothes in the privacy of your home. Below we provide some fast and not-so-hard rules to help you navigate the often strange world of laundromats:

Go on off days and off times. "Saturday or Sunday is probably a good day to wash clothes. I've got nothing else going on." You know what? That's what everybody else in your dorm/

apartment is thinking too. I remember attempting my first wash in the college dorm on a Saturday morning only to find it jampacked. Tuesdays or Wednesdays are good days to go to the laundromat. If your schedule permits, go in the afternoon. If not, become an early-riser and do your laundry first thing in the morning.

Grab plenty of quarters before leaving. Yes, some laundromats and dormitory facilities use credit card or student ID readers these days, but it's a good way to put your change to use, and the change machines at laundromats that lack the credit card option are often broken.

Check washers and dryers before putting your clothes in. A leftover blue sock can turn your whitey-tighties into baby blue under-roos. Also, make sure to clean out the lint screen, but use a paper towel. You don't want to touch the discarded pubes of complete strangers.

Use multiple machines when you can. One of the benefits of going to the laundromat on off days is that you'll likely have access to multiple machines. So instead of washing and drying one load at a time, you can have multiple loads going at once, thus cutting your laundry time down significantly. Of course, you need to be courteous when using this technique. Don't be the guy who hogs three machines when there's a line of other people waiting for an open machine.

Be wary about leaving your laundry unattended. People

steal laundry. Take that into consideration before leaving your laundry unattended. I know you'd probably prefer to be other places besides a laundromat, but I'd recommend hanging around until your clothes are finished. Get some work done while you're waiting or read a book. Make use of that downtime. If you do decide to leave your laundry washing/drying unattended, be sure to set a timer on your phone so you come back right when the cycle is done; don't make someone else take out your laundry and pile it on a table so they can use the machine.

Don't forget your manners. Ask people to move their own laundry if you need space on the tables; nobody likes a strange man handling their intimates. On the same note, don't take up too much space. You don't need to sprawl all your clean clothes out on the table to fold them.

DAY 3

How to Open
and Manage a
Checking Account

For a young man just beginning to establish his financial life, opening a checking account is a small, but important, step in that process. A checking account is the workhorse of your accounts. It's for money that you plan on spending or transferring to another account quickly. Because of the ease at which you can deposit and withdraw from a checking account, it will likely be the hub of all your financial activity.

Below we provide important tips and considerations on opening your first checking account. (While you're at it, open up a savings account for your emergency fund.) For those of you who already have a checking account, we also provide some friendly reminders on managing it wisely.

What to Look for in a Checking Account

Not all checking accounts are created equal. Some banks offer higher-than-average interest rates, while others offer accounts with no interest; some banks charge a monthly fee to keep your money with them, while others offer free checking accounts. Below we highlight a few things to consider when selecting and applying for a checking account:

Look for free checking accounts, but understand that a free checking account isn't really "free." A free checking account is an account that doesn't charge you a monthly service fee to keep your money in that account. Many banks used to offer free checking accounts without any strings attached, but those days are largely over. Now, most banks won't charge you a monthly fee so long as you meet certain conditions. Usually the conditions are that you make a certain amount of direct deposits and debit card transactions each month, or you maintain a certain minimum balance.

If you fail to meet those requirements, the monthly service fee is around $5 at most banks.

Look for accounts with no minimum balance requirement. When you're young and just starting out in life, your cash flow is likely minuscule. When I was in college, it was common for my checking account to dip below $100 despite my best efforts at budgeting. If you have a bank account that requires a minimum balance and you dip below that number, you're going to be slapped with a penalty. Many free checking accounts have no minimum balance requirement (but require you to make direct deposits or debit card transactions to keep the account free), so select one of those.

Avoid checking accounts that offer higher-than-average interest rates. They look enticing, but they usually require a minimum balance of a few thousand dollars.

Look for accounts with online access. You want to keep on top of how much money is coming in and going out of your checking account. It used to be you had to religiously keep track of every single one of your transactions in a check register if you wanted to know how much you had in your account. Today most banks offer free online services that let you check your account online. Get one that does. Also check if your bank allows you to hook up your accounts with services like Mint, YouNeedaBudget, or Quicken. Keeping track of your checkbook on your computer is much easier than using the old pocket register.

Ask how check "holds" are handled. Let's say you get a big fat $2,000 from Grandpa to help pay for school. You deposit it in your account. You're ready to drop a $2,000 money bomb at the bursar's office the next day, right? Nope.

Banks usually place "holds" on checks from other banks (especially out-of-state banks), for a few days to ensure the check or electronic deposit will be honored by the issuing bank. During this hold period, you won't have access to the money you deposited. For checks from local sources, the hold period is usually two days; for out-of-state check sources, the hold period can be up to five days.

It's good to know your bank's policy so you don't spend money that you don't have access to yet.

Get an account with a check/debit card. Most banks offer customers a debit card when they open up an account. Debit cards offer the convenience of credit cards, without the crippling high interest rates. Whenever you swipe a check card, your checking account is deducted.

WHAT'S THE DIFFERENCE BETWEEN CHOOSING CREDIT OR DEBIT ON CHECK CARD READERS?

Whenever you swipe your check card at a store, you'll often be asked to select "credit or debit." While both options will result in money being deducted from your checking account, they each process the transaction differently.

If you select "credit" and your check card happens to be a Visa checking card, your transaction is verified with your signature (sometimes), and will be processed through Visa's networks. The benefit to you for using your debit card as credit is that you get to take advantage of Visa's added security options to prevent against fraudulent transactions. You can also earn reward points with certain cards. Store owners have to pay Visa a pretty hefty service fee (usually 2% of the transaction) every time you choose credit, which is why you may have recently noticed the check card readers at your favorite store bring up debit as the default option, forcing you to press the cancel button, and select credit instead.

If you select "debit," you'll need to enter your four-digit PIN. After you enter it, your transaction will be processed through an electronic funds transfer, and funds are taken from your account instantly. You don't get the same protections on your purchase as you do when you select credit, and debit transactions aren't eligible for reward programs. You can, however, ask for cash back when you make a purchase using debit. That means if your purchase was $5, you can have the store debit your card for $25, and the store will give you $20 straight from the till. That comes in handy when you need cash, but don't want to pay an ATM fee. Be aware that store owners, especially mom and pop places, prefer debit transactions because of the reduced service cost.

Look for a bank with plenty of ATMs in the area and ask about ATM fees. You'll have those days when you need quick access to cash. That's where ATMs will come in handy. But the convenience of ATMs comes at a price. While most banks offer machines that don't charge withdrawal fees for their own customers, banks will charge you a fee for using a competitor's ATM. When you add that fee, to the fee or surcharge the competitor's bank charges you to use their ATM, you're looking at paying about $5 just to get your cash.

SHOULD I GO WITH AN ONLINE-ONLY BANK?

In the past few years, the number of online-only banks has increased dramatically. Because they have less overhead than brick and mortar banks, online banks are able to provide higher interest rates and charge fewer fees. A few years ago, online banks like CapitalOne 360 and Ally had crazy monthly interest rates between 2%-4%, but they've since gone down to about 0.8%-1%. Not fantastic, but still better than most traditional banks.

While checking accounts from online banks provide higher interest rates than traditional banks, I'd still open your first checking account with a traditional bank. Here's why:

Things take longer to clear with online accounts. The internet is supposed to make things faster. Online banks didn't get the memo. Checks and even electronic deposits, however big or small, take forever to clear online banks. For example, when I make transfers from my main checking account to my emergency fund that I keep in an online CapitalOne checking account, it takes about three days before I have access to that money. For large deposits or transfers, the wait is longer. Not good if you need money to clear fast.

You can't easily deposit paper checks or cash with online accounts. If you ever get a check or cash for your birthday from Aunt Gertrude, depositing that money into your online banking account can be tricky. Most online banks require all your transactions to be electronic. But there are some that allow you to mail in the check or cash. Even if you can mail the paper check, it will be a while before you have access to that money — you have to wait for the check to arrive at the online bank's headquarters, and then you have to wait another couple of days before the check clears.

However, some online banks are beginning to provide services that allow you to deposit a check from anywhere by simply snapping a photo of the check with your smartphone, so this is changing.

Many online banks also don't provide wire services or cashier's checks. That can get you into trouble when you're buying a car or a home (or posting bond to get someone out of jail!), as those transactions often require a cashier's check. If all your money is in an online bank on closing day, you're sunk.

You get better service with traditional banks. The

only customer service you get with online banks comes by phone or email, but there are some issues that are more easily done face-to-face with a teller. Traditional banks also typically have a network of fee-free ATMs in your area; not so with online banks.

WHAT YOU'LL NEED TO OPEN A CHECKING ACCOUNT

Opening a checking account is a breeze. Just walk into the bank and inform the teller that you'd like to open an account. All you have to do is fill out a short application, show the teller your photo ID, and deposit some money to open up an account. The amount you have to initially deposit will vary from bank to bank — some require only $1, while others ask for $50, $100, or even $250.

Some banks even let you open up an account online, but you'll have to have an account at another institution that you can use to fund your new account.

HOW TO WRITE A CHECK

Because we don't typically write checks every day, when it comes time to do so, it's easy to mess up. Here's how you do it:

1. Always date your checks.

2. Write the name of the person or business you're paying next to "Pay to the order of."

3. Write the amount of the check in numeric format. You should start as far over to the left as possible. This prevents anybody from slipping in an extra number or two.

4. Write out the amount of the check in words. For cents, use a fraction, with 100 as the denominator. In this example since it was $500 even, I wrote out "00/100."

5. Sign the check.

6. It's a good idea to write a short note on what the check was for. It helps with accounting.

MANAGING YOUR CHECKING ACCOUNT

Now that you have a checking account, it's important that you manage it effectively. If you don't keep on top of the money coming and going from your account, you risk the embarrassment and financial penalties that come from spending money you don't have.

Opt-out of overdraft protection. Overdraft protection means that if you make a purchase with your debit card, and you don't have enough money in your account to complete the transaction, the bank will "loan" you the money…and charge you a $25-$35 fee for their "generosity." But that's a big price to pay to avoid the embarrassment or inconvenience of having your card declined or a check bounce. And these fees can add up fast, because here's what many consumers don't know: most banks will purposefully process your largest transactions first, and then your smaller transactions after that. So let's say you have $285 in your checking account, and you buy a coffee for $3.50 in the morning, a sandwich for $5 at noon, and then some college textbooks in the afternoon for $300. The banks will process the $300 transaction first, even though it was made later in the day, thus depleting your account, and then charge you a $35 overdraft fee for the textbooks, another $35 fee for the sandwich, and another $35 for the coffee, and bill you for $105 in total overdraft fees. Ouch!

Banks used to automatically enroll their customers in overdraft protection programs, but a court ruling in 2010 made that illegal. You can and should opt out of overdraft protection. But because overdraft fees were a big moneymaker for banks, they still aggressively try to get you to sign up. Every time I check my bank account online, I get a pop-up that asks if I'm sure I don't want to enroll in their overdraft protection program. You just have to say no and keep saying no.

Check your account weekly. Make a habit of checking your account online every week. Not only does this keep you abreast of how much you have in your account so you don't overspend, it gives you a chance to check for errors or fraudulent transactions. If you notice any errors or possible fraudulent transactions, notify your bank immediately.

Also, sometimes when you have something set up on autopay, like a gym membership or Netflix, that makes a withdrawal from your checking account every month, even when you cancel the service, they can "forget" to stop charging your account. Be on the lookout for this.

Understand that the balance your bank statement says you have could actually be more than you really have. This is something that trips up a lot of young people when they first get a checking account. Your bank says you have $750 in your checking account, so you pay your $500 rent. A few days later you get notice from your bank that you're being charged an overdraft fee and you have an account balance of negative $50. What happened?

Well, a week earlier you wrote a check for $300 for tuition, but it still hadn't cleared when you checked your account. After you sent a check to your landlord, the tuition finally cleared, leaving you in the hole and facing a stiff overdraft fee.

Because of the delay between the moment the transaction occurs and when it actually posts, it's important to track all your debit card transactions, ATM withdrawals, and checks written in a check register. (You can use the old fashioned paper registers or a digital one like Quicken, YouNeedABudget, or Mint. I even know some folks who use a simple Excel spreadsheet.) A check register lets you know how much you really have available in your account. Don't think you can mentally keep track of it. At some point you'll experience a brain fart. I know from experience.

Set up online alerts for when your balance reaches a certain level. To play it safe, establish a base amount for your checking account that you'll never go under. That small amount acts like a firewall for bounced checks. Take it a step further by setting up an alert with your bank's online system that will notify you whenever your checking account balance gets within $50 of your minimum balance. Once you get the alert, cut back on spending and deposit some money.

Use direct deposit for your paychecks and pay bills online. Whenever you land a job, ask your employer to automatically deposit your paychecks into your checking account. You'll have to sign a form and provide a voided check to get auto-deposits set up. Where available, pay as many of your bills online as you can and make them automatic. We'll be talking more about that later in the book.

Balance your checkbook monthly. You've probably seen your parents balance their checkbooks. Balancing a checkbook simply means reconciling the balance your bank says you have in your account with the balance you have in your records. Remember, with the delays between checks clearing, those numbers can be off.

People are divided on whether you need to balance a checkbook in our world of digital finances. But even with the speed of digital transactions, things can get off-kilter in your account, so it's not a bad idea to reconcile your account at least once a month. Money software like Quicken and YouNeedaBudget makes this process a breeze. They'll automatically reconcile your accounts with the click of a button. Sometimes, though, you'll need to bust out the old pen and paper to do some figurin'.

DAY 4

Keep a Regular
Grooming and Hygiene
Routine

———•———

I know. I know. You're probably thinking, "Does Brett think all young men are a bunch of uncouth ignoramuses who need a chapter reminding them to practice basic hygiene?" No. No, I don't.

But from my own personal experience and observing the lives of young men heading out on their own for the first time, I do know that keeping up with regular hygiene practices falls to the wayside for many gents. With the stress of school and work, along with the lack of structure they once had at home, it's easy to let yourself go.

This chapter is simply a friendly reminder to keep up those regular grooming habits you hopefully formed in your youth. If you haven't developed these habits yet, now is a good time to start. You'll feel more alert, have more confidence, and won't repel the ladies. As an added bonus, maintaining good bodily hygiene can help you become a man of character like Benjamin Franklin; cleanliness was one of his 13 core virtues.

Let me be clear. I'm in no way suggesting you become overly fastidious about your personal grooming and hygiene. That sort of preening isn't attractive in a man, and you probably have better things to be doing than standing in the mirror worrying about blemishes. All I'm encouraging is keeping up with the basic stuff you learned in elementary school health class that will keep you smelling fresh and looking presentable.

Brush and floss every day, morning and night. This was the first habit that I let slip when I went away from home the first time. Between waking up late for class and staying up late into the evening playing video games, my morning and evening dental care became pretty irregular. But I paid for my negligence by having to get two cavities filled at the end of the semester. What a preventable waste of money.

Invest three minutes of your day, morning and night, into proper dental hygiene. Brush twice a day, floss once. Even if you're dog tired and ready to go to bed, make the effort to get it done. Include a tongue scraping in your routine, too. That really helps in decreasing bad breath. Taking care of your oral hygiene is a habit that will save you money in the long run and increase the chances for that kiss at the end of a date.

Shower regularly. You'll have that occasional string of days when you're so busy that you don't have time to shower. But don't let your showerlessness go on for more than three days. If you get a job in a restaurant, it's important to shower after every shift, unless of course you're dating someone who enjoys nuzzling a man who smells like refried beans.

I've had several young folks ask me if there's some sort of special "manly" soap or shampoo they should use. Grandpa's Pine Tar Soap is a favorite of mine. You can find it at most health food stores. You can use it on both your skin and hair, it's supposed to help with everything from psoriasis to dandruff, and it leaves you smelling like a basement in Vermont…in the best possible way. But really, your soap choice doesn't matter, even though there's a bunch of new marketing and "men's-only" soaps and shampoos telling you otherwise. Get the giant econo-pack of Irish Spring and you're good to go. If you have very sensitive or acne-prone skin, get a special facial soap for those needs.

Go easy on the cologne. Body sprays are heavily marketed to young men as a foolproof way to attract the ladies, leading some guys to go overboard by enveloping themselves in a cloud of it before going out. Instead, apply just a couple of dabs or sprays of cologne to areas like your neck or the insides of your wrists. For a young man on a budget, colognes need not be any more expensive than body sprays — there are many drugstore varieties that only cost a few bucks and have very appealing and masculine scents.

Make friends with Gold Bond Powder. Nothing keeps away the swamp crotch and stinky feet like Gold Bond Powder. If you live in hot, humid climates, Gold Bond is a must. Just sprinkle some on your junk and in your shoes. You'll stay cool and dry all day long.

Keep your nails trimmed. Unless you're a flamenco guitarist or going for a Guinness World Record, keep your fingernails trimmed. Don't chew them; gnawed up nails are not attractive and give some people the heebie-jeebies. Get a simple nail clipper and give your nails a quick trim once a week before you hop into the shower. Follow the natural curve of your finger as you cut, leaving the thin, white, unattached crescent of the nail about as wide as a dime. Just enough to still scratch your head.

It's important to keep your toenails trimmed, too, especially since flips-flops are incredibly popular footwear for young men. You don't want to look like a sloth or scrape your woman's legs with your claws when you're canoodling. But don't go overboard with the toenail trimming. Excessive trimming can lead to ingrown toenails. Cut straight across the nail and leave them a little long. Toenails that are cut too short are prone to burrowing back into your flesh.

Whether you're trimming your fingernails or toenails, be sure to clean up afterwards — don't leave your trimmings on the floor or countertop. If you've got dirt under your nails, scoop it out with the nail file that is probably attached to your clippers. And if you get a hangnail, carefully clip it off, rather than pulling at it and making it bleed.

Unless you have extended-wear contacts, take your contacts out every night. Sleeping with your contacts in several nights in a row makes you susceptible to corneal ulcers. I know a guy who got 'em because he never took his contacts out. Even with extended-wear contacts, my optometrist told me it's still not a good idea to wear them while sleeping for more than a few nights in a row.

Shave regularly/keep facial hair groomed. College is a time when many young men start experimenting with facial hair. Nothing wrong with that at all. But whether you go with a full-on beard or a distinguished mustache, commit to it and keep it groomed. Don't be one of those guys who grows a patchy neckbeard every two weeks because he's too lazy to shave. Two days of scruff can be attractive. Two weeks of ungroomed, patchy neckbeard growth looks gross. If you're going to go neckbeard, do it right, and look up a photo of Henry David Thoreau.

When it comes to shaving, if you've grown up using a cartridge razor, now's a good time to experiment with using a safety razor and making shaving more of an enjoyable ritual in your life. We've written about this topic on our site, so be sure to check it out at this URL: *http://www.artofmanliness. com/2008/01/04/how-to-shave-like-your-grandpa/*

Keep your hair trimmed. Just as with facial hair, college is a time where guys both experiment with growing their hair out and get kind of lazy with taking care of it. Letting your hair get a little shaggy is a normal part of the college experience. But don't let it get totally out of hand; it's time for a trim when it becomes a distraction to you. I didn't get my hair cut at all my first semester, and my hair, which is naturally quite thick and ample, became a giant, unattractive bowl that made me feel nappy and disheveled. When your hair is getting in your eyes and stuff, it's time for a haircut. What, what's that you say? Some young men purposefully grow out Bieber-esque bangs that they swing from side to side and push out of their eyes every few minutes? Why would a man want to mess with his hair that much? What's that you say? I sound like an old man? Yes, yes I do.

By the way, just as now is a good time to try shaving with a safety razor, if you've only gotten your haircut at Supercuts growing up, now's a good time to start taking part in the manly ritual of visiting a local barbershop. Get some friends together and go try it.

Treat your acne. Having acne can make you feel really

self-conscious and sap your self-confidence. But in this day and age, it's easily treatable in the vast majority of cases, and there's absolutely no need to suffer through it. If you've got a mild case, wash your face morning and night with a face wash made for acne-prone skin and spot treat pimples with a benzoyl peroxide cream when they pop up. If that dries out your skin, use a face wash for acne-prone skin once a day, and a gentle cleanser like Cetaphil once a day. If you get more than an occasional pimple, you might be tempted to try something like Proactiv, but there are much cheaper alternatives out there. Proactiv basically consists of a face wash and topical treatment in which the active ingredient is benzoyl peroxide. But you can buy generic benzoyl peroxide face washes and creams separately at the drugstore for a fraction of the cost. Try that first. Keep in mind that benzoyl peroxide can bleach your clothes and pillowcase, so wash the cream off your fingers after you apply it, and don't put it on during the day, as it can sweat into the collar of your colored shirt. Use a white pillow case at home, and remember this when you visit someone!

It can also help to get a short haircut that keeps the hair off your face and skin (see, not just an old man thing – there are truly practical reasons for keeping it short!) and to wash your pillowcase regularly.

If your acne doesn't clear up, don't hesitate to visit your doctor, as they can prescribe antibiotics and topical treatments that can clear up your face entirely.

Finally, if you've got bacne, here's a post we've written about how to deal with it: *www.artofmanliness.com/2009/10/21/ battling-bacne*

Wash your hands. A 2005 survey at ballparks indicated that 37 percent of men didn't wash their hands after using the restroom. Gross. If you want to stay healthy, especially during cold and flu season, wash your hands regularly. I always disregarded this injunction too, until one semester in college I came down with a flu that left me with it coming out of both ends, and stuck shivering and feverish in bed for several days; I couldn't do anything fun, or workout, or study, even though I really needed to. It sucked big time and wasted a week of my life. After that experience, I became better at hand-washing.

On a related note...get a flu shot every year. If you're a student, your school might offer them for free at the student health center, otherwise you can get them for $25 at Walgreens. It's one of the best investments you can make...you can't put a price on a whole week of your life.

DAY 5

Create a Weekly
Attack Plan

Growing up, each day is pretty well-scheduled out for you. School from morning til afternoon. After school sports or a job. Homework. Time for bed. Once you leave home for the first time, all that structure is gone; it is up to you to shape each day and get things done. It's an open plain of freedom, and the way is so broad that many young men get completely lost.

It happened to me. One of the things I struggled with the most my first few months away from home was managing my time. I pretty much was flying by the seat of my pants every day. Things in my life started falling between the cracks very quickly, and I soon found myself struggling beneath an overwhelming pile of to-dos and obligations.

Things turned around for me as soon as I instituted a new habit: weekly planning. Stephen Covey's (R.I.P.) *First Things First* was the catalyst for the change. When I got to law school, my weekly planning sessions became even more crucial. The rigors of my legal studies on top of my work on the law review and the Art of Manliness required that I had my days planned to the minute so that I could get everything done.

The power of weekly planning lies in the perspective and control it provides for your life; instead of drifting along, you give yourself a bird's-eye view of the maze below, and harness your newfound freedom in order to do, be, and get wherever you want to go. It allows you to manage the day-to-day and often trivial tasks along with your long-term plans and goals. Think of your weekly calendar as an Attack Plan for Life: it's where you hash out the tactics and logistics to make your long-term vision a reality.

Below I share how I go about my Weekly Attack Plan sessions. It's sort of a mishmash of time and task management ideas from Stephen Covey and David Allen. I don't claim that it's the best way to plan your week, but it's worked for me. Maybe it will work for you too, or at least inspire you to come up with you own system.

Establish Your Attack Plan Day & Set Aside an Hour to Plan

Pick a day that you'll use to establish your Weekly Attack Plan. The weekend is a good time to do it because it allows you to both review the previous week's successes and failures and look ahead to the next week. I do mine on Sunday. I know some folks who do theirs on Friday. Pick whichever day works best for you.

Set aside about an hour on your chosen day for planning. The first few times you execute a Weekly Attack Plan session it may take you longer, but that's okay. After a while, you'll establish a rhythm that will allow you to breeze through it in about 45 minutes.

Go somewhere where you can be alone and away from distractions. I like to do my weekly planning sessions on Sunday nights in our home office. When I was in college, I'd go to a quiet corner of the Student Union.

Pick Your Calendaring Tool

Everyone has their own preference for what to use for calendaring. Some people prefer digital calendaring tools like iCalendar, Outlook, or Google Calendar; others prefer using good old-fashioned pencil and paper to plan.

Each format has pros and cons. Digital calendars make planning re-occurring events a breeze. They also can send friendly reminders to you via email or simply as a pop-up on smartphone screens a few minutes before your event. It's kind of like having a personal assistant. Many digital calendars also allow you to share calendars with others, which can come in handy when trying to sync multiple schedules.

The downside of digital calendars, in my experience, is that they're kind of a pain when it comes to adding new events, especially on your smartphone's tiny keypad. You have to type in the event, select the time, and decide if you want a reminder. Granted, once an event is created, moving things around is a snap — just point and click.

Voice recognition software is beginning to eliminate this problem, but sometimes there are still goofs. Digital calendars also share a downside common to all digital tools: if your device runs out of power, you can't access your calendar.

With paper and pencil calendars, you don't have to worry about running out of power. When you want to add a new event, you can scribble it down in seconds. There's also something about the tactile nature of planning with pencil and paper that really gets your strategic juices going. And because we're on our phones and computers so much these days, it's nice to give your brain a break with something different. But there are a few downsides to paper and pencil calendars. If you lose your calendar, you're sunk. Unlike digital calendars that exist eternally in the "cloud," when you lose a pencil and paper calendar, you'll have to recreate it from memory. You don't get any email reminders about upcoming events with an analog calendar. And if you have re-occurring events, you'll have to write them out every. single. week. on a new weekly calendar.

I used to be a pencil and paper planner guy, but switched to digital calendaring tools this year. I like having everything synced up across all my devices. Experiment with the different calendaring tools out there and pick the one that's comfortable for you. If you're looking for a good pencil and paper weekly calendar, you can download the one I created for myself when I was in law school at this URL: *http://bit.ly/1cL66My*

PERFORM A MIND DUMP TO FREE-UP MENTAL RAM

During the week, our minds build up a giant list of stuff that needs to be done: call mom back, do the laundry, respond to your backlog of emails, study, etc. The problem with these loose ends camping on our craniums is that they're subtly eating up our willpower, causing us to feel stressed out and mentally fatigued.

These unfinished mental tasks are like programs you have running on your computer, but aren't actually using. We've all had those moments working on our computer when the fan is running full blast, and everything seems to be taking an eternity to load. You check the Activity Monitor only to see that a bunch of unused apps are hogging a crapload of memory, causing your World of Warcraft raid to screech to a halt. Just as unused computer programs use up precious RAM and slow down your computer, so too do unfinished tasks use up willpower and slow down your brain.

Free up some mental RAM and get your brain running on all six cylinders again by performing a mind dump. A mind dump is exactly what it sounds like: you get everything out of your head and onto paper (or a computer screen). You can actually feel your brain let out a sigh of relief as you write down the stuff it's been spending precious willpower trying to remember.

Use whatever tool you're comfortable with for a mind dump. It doesn't matter. I know several people who use a notebook and pen and others who use digital tools like OmniFocus, Things, Nozbe, or Evernote to capture their mind dump (I use Things). The important thing is simply that you have someplace to store all that stuff.

Once you settle on a capture tool, simply start writing or typing all the tasks, ideas, and commitments that have been weighing you down during the previous week. If you need some nudging on the types of open loops you might having running in your mental background, check out the "trigger" list from David Allen's *Getting Things Done* (it can also be found online). It's like a laxative for your brain. Just go down the list and capture any unfinished tasks that come to you as you read through it.

We'll schedule items from our mind dump later.

REVIEW YOUR LIFE PLAN & GOALS

Now that we've detoxed our brains and freed up some mental RAM, it's time to review our life plan and long-term goals. This step will help you keep "first things first" in mind as you plan your week out and ensure you're staying on track with your long-term goals. Sure, you may have been successful in completing your short-term goals, but if those short-term goals get you off track with your future aims, what good are they? If needed, reevaluate your short-term to-do list in light of your long-term goals. You might need to amend your life plan and goals as well, as new experiences and insights change your vision of where you want to be down the road.

Don't have a life plan or goals? Well, now's the time to create them. To learn how, check out our comprehensive guide on creating a life plan: *www.artofmanliness.com/2011/02/08/create-a-life-plan*

REVIEW THE PREVIOUS WEEK

Reflect on your previous week and how you performed in your various roles as a man. How did it go? Did you achieve the goals you set for yourself? What were your successes and failures? How could you have done things differently? Any tasks or items you need to follow-up on? I recommend writing down any thoughts that come to you during your reflection on the previous week in a journal. First, the act of writing helps make your thoughts more concrete and well thought-out. Second, by writing down your observations about the previous week, you create a record that you can look back on to see if you're improving.

SET WEEKLY GOALS

After I've reviewed my previous week, I start setting goals for the coming one. I use Stephen Covey's role-based goal-setting method, but if you have a method that works better for you, use it.

Here's how the role-based goal-setting method works. When I created my life plan, I defined and prioritized the different roles I fill as a man: husband, father, brother/son, friend, writer, and business owner. Your roles might be student, friend, roommate, boyfriend, etc. Every week I create a goal that I want to accomplish within each role. So for example, a goal for my role as a husband could be to write Kate a love note or take her on a date; a goal for my role as a writer could be to check out and read a book about improving my writing.

I also follow Covey's advice on creating weekly "Sharpening the Saw" goals. As you saw away at your goals, the blade is going to become dull — you have to take the time to sharpen it up. Thus Sharpening the Saw goals are all about keeping yourself sharp in all aspects of your life: physically, mentally, socially/emotionally, and spiritually. I try to create a weekly goal for improvement in all of those four areas. A weekly physical goal could be to bench press x-amount of weight; a mental goal could be to read a book or listen to a lecture on your commute to work; a social goal could be to write your college bud a letter; and a spiritual goal could be to meditate every day for 15 minutes.

Lay a Foundation for Success With Re-occurring Time Blocks

After I've set my goals for the coming week, I move on to putting them in my calendar. I first block out time on my weekly schedule for my Sharpening the Saw goals. These are small and simple things that keep me feeling sharp no matter what sort of chaos happens during the week. So I have time blocked off for exercising, reading, and prayer and meditation. An important part of keeping your saw sharp is weekly and daily planning, so I block time off for it, too. I treat these events like a doctor's appointment — I don't schedule anything else during these times and don't deviate from them unless it's an emergency. I've blocked time off every day in the week for these activities and have my iCal programmed so that they repeat every week.

Block Out Time for Your "Big Rocks"

In his book, *First Things First*, Stephen Covey introduced a really clever object lesson on how to get more done in life, while ensuring you actually accomplish your most important and meaningful tasks. From *First Things First*:

> I attended a seminar once where the instructor was lecturing on time. At one point, he said, "Okay, it's time for a quiz." He reached under the table and pulled out a wide-mouth gallon jar. He set it on the table next to a platter with some fist-sized rocks on it. "How many of these rocks do you think we can get in the jar?" he asked.

After we made our guess, he said, "Okay. Let's find out."

He set one rock in the jar…then another…then another. I don't remember how many he got in, but he got the jar full. Then he asked, "Is the jar full?"

Everybody looked at the rocks and said, "Yes."

Then he said, "Ahhh." He reached under the table and pulled out a bucket of gravel. Then he dumped some gravel in and shook the jar and the gravel went in all the little spaces left by the big rocks. Then he grinned and said once more, "Is the jar full?"

By this time we were on to him. "Probably not," we said.

"Good!" he replied. And he reached under the table and brought out a bucket of sand. He started dumping the sand in and it went in all the little spaces left by the rocks and the gravel. Once more he looked at us and said, "Is the jar full?"

"No!" we all roared.

He said, "Good!" and he grabbed a pitcher of water and began to pour it in. He got something like a quart of water in that jar. Then he said, "Well, what's the point?"

Somebody said, "Well, there are gaps and if you really work at it, you can always fit more into your life."

"No," he said, "that's not the point. The point is this: if you hadn't put these big rocks in first, would you ever have gotten any of them in?"

Most young men fill their schedules with the gravel, sand, and water of life first. Sure, these men look and feel busy, but all they ever work on are the small tasks that are likely inconsequential in the long run. You'll find these sorts of gents wistfully lamenting that they never have time for the things that are truly important in life: the Big Rocks.

What the object lesson above teaches us is that if we want to accomplish our most important goals and tasks, we need to put them in our schedule first. Those smaller tasks can get done during the gaps between your Big Rocks.

What's a Big Rock? It's going to be different for every man. Look at your mind dump list and pick three or four items that you consider to be your MITs: most important tasks.

If you're a student, one of your MITs is definitely your education. To ensure that you actually make school a priority, block off time during the week for the following activities:

1. Block off your class and lab times. The most important appointments of your week. Schedule everything else around your class times.

2. Block off reading time for each of your classes. If you have a Monday/Wednesday/Friday schedule, you'll probably want to block off an hour or two on Sunday/Tuesday/Thursday for reading.

3. Block off time for note review/outlining/homework for each class. You'll want to set aside time so you can synthesize class notes, do some outlining, and complete any homework assignments you might have. I typically blocked off an hour right after each class for this. If a class was lecture heavy, like ancient Greek philosophy, I'd use that hour right after class to review my notes and update my class outline. If the class was heavy on problem sets, like calculus or symbolic logic, I used the hour to do that day's assignment and any additional practice problems.

The amount of time you need for note review/outlining/homework will vary. I recommend setting aside at least one hour for each hour spent in class. If you need more time, schedule it.

No matter what your personal Big Rocks are, block off a set amount of time on your calendar to work on them and don't let anything bump them from your schedule. Remember: Big Rocks first!

BLOCK OUT TIME FOR OTHER TASKS

Take a look at your list of items you captured during your Mind Dump and block out time to accomplish those tasks. So if you need to get the oil on your car changed or make a gift for your girlfriend's birthday, block off a time on your schedule to complete those tasks.

How do you know which tasks on your Mind Dump list to tackle first? You can use a system where your go through and rate them by importance with "A, B, C," or something similar, and then schedule the A's to be completed first. But I have personally found that what is most important jumps right out at me as I look over the list.

My goal by the end of my planning sessions is to have every one of my waking hours of every day of the week blocked out with something. Don't get the wrong idea. I'm not constantly doing something every minute of the day — I schedule time for doing absolutely nothing, too — but I like to have at least an outline of how I'm going to spend my time during the week. I consider my completely filled-in weekly calendar just a rough draft of my week and expect to edit and adjust during my daily planning sessions. Which leads me to…

REVIEW AND ADJUST YOUR WEEKLY ATTACK PLAN DAILY

Even the best laid plans need adjusting. That's why daily planning is so important. Every evening, I'll review my calendar and make adjustments as needed. While I try to avoid rescheduling my Sharpen the Saw and Big Rock events, I move around the other tasks I scheduled during my Weekly Attack Plan session with gusto. Do likewise.

DO IT AGAIN NEXT WEEK (AND THE WEEK AFTER THAT, AND THE WEEK AFTER…)

If you want to see success come from your Weekly Attack Plan sessions, you have to do them consistently. I'll admit that I've had my moments where I've fallen off the wagon on it. Kate can usually tell when I haven't been planning my week out, because I get unproductive and grouchy — totally off my game. I just don't function well without the structure of a weekly plan.

I promise as you consistently plan out your week, you'll find yourself with more motivation, direction, and peace in your life.

DAY 6

How to Ace
a Job Interview

———•———

Nearly every man will go through at least one job interview at some point, maybe even several dozen over his lifetime. Even if you plan on becoming an entrepreneur and your own boss, many businesses start off as a side hustle to your 9-5 before becoming a full-time gig, and plenty of millionaires spent time in their younger years waiting tables and filing papers.

Knowing how to ace a job interview is a skill every man can master. There are numerous ways to hone that skill and special considerations for different kinds of interviews, and we'll definitely cover those specific ins and outs down the road on the blog. But for now, we present the most important basics for job interview success — these essentials work whether you're applying for a job at a Pizza Hut or a law firm.

Clean-up your online presence. Many employers are using the internet to screen job applicants. And it's not just big corporations that are doing this. I know a manager of a restaurant here in town that checks the public Facebook profiles of people who submit applications. What are employers looking for? They're looking for any red flags that indicate you might be a bad employee — pictures of you toking it up or funneling beer, or status updates where you use excessively crude language or bad mouth a former/current employer will probably land your application in the trash.

We'll be going into more detail about how to clean-up and manage your online reputation later in the book. Stay tuned.

Have a list of references that your interviewer can actually call. Every job application you submit, whether for the local ice cream parlor or a fancy corporation, will probably ask for a list of references. While many hiring managers don't actually call the references you give, in the off chance that they do, you want your references to be people that can honestly put in a good word for you. Before you list a person as a reference, shoot them an email and ask if you can use them as a reference. That way, if they do get a call from an employer, they'll be prepared and won't be stammering to come up with something good to say about you, let alone remember who you were.

Research the employer. Know something about the company or business you're applying for. First, you want to know that the job and working environment is a good fit for you. Second, you want to be prepared to answer questions like: "Why do you want to work here?" or "What do you know about our company?" Third, knowing a lot about the company will enable you to ask your own questions about the job, which is a key way to impress the interviewer (see below).

Know your resume and what you wrote down on your application. If you're applying for a job that requires you to submit a resume, have everything you put in your resume down pat and be prepared to elaborate if asked. Same goes for anything you put on a job application. Be prepared to answer any questions about what you put down.

And it should go without saying, but be completely honest with what you put on your resume or application. I know one young woman in law school who put on her resume that she spoke Spanish fluently, which in reality meant she had taken three years of college Spanish and could sort of stumble through a very rudimentary conversation. Little did she know that the hiring attorney had lived in Spain for several years and spoke Spanish like a native. After a few minutes of questions, the hiring attorney started asking her questions in Spanish. She had no idea what he was saying. Needless to say, she didn't get a second interview.

Dress appropriately. You want to put your best foot forward during your interview, and your appearance is a big part of that. It's the first part of your first impression. You want to look presentable, well-groomed, and dressed appropriately for the type of job you're applying for.

Just use some common sense when determining what to wear to the interview. A good general rule to follow is to dress one notch up from how people who already work there dress. So if you're applying to a restaurant where the waiters wear jeans and t-shirts, wear khakis and a polo shirt to the interview. If you're applying to a place where people wear khakis and polos, then wear a button-down shirt and khakis to the interview. If everyone wears khakis and button-down shirts, then do likewise, but add a sport coat and tie. You get the idea.

Be punctual. If you're applying to a part-time wage job, one of the most important attributes an employer is looking for in an employee is reliability. Every employer will tell you…reliable people are hard to find! Employers want to know the people they hire will show up for the shift they're assigned to, at the time they're scheduled, and will come in ready to work. If you stroll into your interview late, what do you think that tells the employer? That you'll likely be a tardy employee.

Practice the manly art of punctuality. Show up 5-10 minutes early (more if it's a professional job with a waiting area, less if it's a casual job with no place for you to wait), let somebody know that you're there for your interview, and wait until the manager is ready for you. If you're running late because of an emergency, call the interviewer and let them know.

If the manager makes you wait, don't act perturbed. That's their prerogative. Just keep being your pleasant self. When the manager finally comes and gets you and apologizes for making you wait, act like it wasn't a big deal at all, even if you had to wait 15 minutes. Of course, you should take into account a manager's tardiness when determining if you'll accept a job offer. Having an unreliable boss can make a job a pain.

Understand that the interview begins as soon as you walk through the door. As soon as you walk through the door, the interview has started. Assume that everyone you encounter before and after you meet the hiring manager will have a say in whether you get the job or not. And by everyone, I mean everyone: janitors, secretaries, hostesses, and customers included. Hiring managers often ask their subordinates what they thought of job applicants. If you were rude to the secretary or cold and aloof with the hostess at the restaurant, kiss your chances of landing the job goodbye. Treat everyone with the utmost respect and be your best self.

Shake hands, smile, and look the employer in the eye. Display confidence during your interview. As soon as you see the hiring manager walk towards you, stand up and walk towards her with a smile and an open hand. Give a firm handshake and say, "Nice to meet you!" Follow the hiring manager to where the interview will take place and don't sit until she says, "Take a seat."

Sit comfortably and straight in your chair. Sit up straight, but comfortably straight. You don't want to look like a robot. Don't cross your arms in front of you — that makes you look defensive. Just rest them gently on your thighs. Don't be afraid to gesture as you answer questions — it shows you're excited. Avoid any nervous ticks like checking your watch, tapping your foot, or touching your face and hair.

Show excitement and interest. As someone who has been on the other side of the desk in conducting job interviews, nothing is worse than talking to someone who shows no interest or excitement about the job. All I'm thinking is: "Why am I wasting my time with this person who doesn't even want to be here?" So cleaning bathrooms isn't the most exciting job in the world. If you want the job, you darn well better act like there's nothing you'd rather do than clean bathrooms. Remember this: job interviews are a form of theater and everyone has a role to play. Your role is "eager job applicant who is ready to roll up his sleeves and get to work, even if the work isn't all that glamorous."

Keep answers brief (but not too brief). Don't just give one-word answers, but don't keep blabbing on and on. Answers to most basic interview questions shouldn't take more than a minute to answer.

Rehearse answers to common interview questions. Again, job interviews are a form of theater. Just as you'd rehearse your lines for a play, so too should you rehearse your lines for a job interview. There are plenty of websites with huge lists of common job interview questions. Print them off and rehearse them by yourself and with a friend in a mock interview. Below I highlight a few of the most common interview questions and offer some suggestions on how to answer them:

> **"Tell me about yourself."** I hate this question because it's so incredibly broad. But interviewers like to ask it because it shows how you to handle unstructured situations, so you might as well be ready for it. Whatever you do, don't respond with: "What do you want to know?" Nor should you launch into your life story…"Well, I was born in McAllen, Texas, and I have a dog named Mabel…" Despite how the question is worded, employers don't actually want to know about you — *they want to know something about you that's relevant to the open job.* Tell them why you're applying for this job and highlight any strengths that you'll bring to the business. "I'm a freshman at the University of Oklahoma studying history. I worked as a waiter this summer in Edmond, and now that I'm living in Norman, I'm looking for another job

waiting tables. I think I've got the kind of enthusiastic personality that would fit really well with your restaurant."

"What are your strengths?" Pick two or three of your biggest strengths and have a few specific examples that offer a concrete and memorable demonstration of those qualities.

"What are your weaknesses?" Don't say, "I can't think of any." Don't go the cliche "here's a weakness that's actually kind of a strength" route ("I'm too much of a perfectionist!"). And don't overshare. This isn't a time to confess your weird habits. Come up with one thing that isn't a huge deal, and then — here's the important part — explain what you're doing to correct it. This is what employers are trying to get at with this question. They want to see if you're self-aware enough to see deficiencies in yourself and that you're able to take actions to correct them. So you might say, "I used to be really unorganized and scatter-brained. That was okay in high school, but this first semester in college my grades started to suffer. So I started studying about productivity and time management and now I plan my weeks and days out religiously. I've never been more on the ball."

"I see you don't have any experience in _____. Why do you think you would succeed in this position?" If this is the first job you've ever applied for or it's a job in a field you have no experience in, this question can throw you for a loop. If you don't have any experience in the position you're applying for, look for skills you've demonstrated in other areas of your life that can crossover to the job. Have you done community service? Were you the captain of your cross-country team? Did you help plan the prom? Did you take care of your sick grandfather? Use experiences from all areas of your life to show you're prepared for the job.

Have some questions for the interviewer ready. Interviewers usually finish things up by asking, "So do you have any questions for *us*?" The incorrect response is, "Nope! You answered all my questions."

Always have some thoughtful questions ready to ask the hiring manager. Again, it shows that you're interested in the job. Moreover, it demonstrates that you're not a potato head and that you actually have the brain power to formulate a thoughtful question. Most importantly, it's your chance to find out if the job really is a good fit for *you*.

Here are some possible questions to ask about the job:

- "What characteristics does your ideal employee have?"
- "What's the culture like here?"
- "Why do people like to work here?"
- "What's the training like?"
- If you're applying for a service job, ask whether the business experiences any "rushes" and how they handle them.
- "What's the next step? When will you be making a decision? Can I follow up with you in a week?"

While you should definitely ask your interviewer questions, don't ask a question that he already answered during the course of the interview. So, if the employer gave a rundown of your potential job duties at the beginning of the interview, don't ask, "So what will I be doing here?" at the end of it. You just demonstrated that you suck at paying attention. Also avoid questions that make you look lazy or that might raise red flags; for example, "Um, do you do background checks?" or, "How soon can I ask for time off?"

Thank the interviewer for their time. When the interview is finished, shake the interviewer's hand, and thank him for his time. Make it sincere. Last impressions count nearly as much as first ones do. If it's a more professional job, and one you really want, stick a thank you note in the mail the same day as the interview. Some folks say the thank you note is outdated these days and just to send an email. But personally, if I got such an email, I'd think, "Yes, I know. You just thanked me a few hours ago." An email is about on the same level as an in-person thank you, so it seems redundant. And most people get so much email, they really don't look forward to more. They'll forget about it in the time it takes to click *delete*. A handwritten note, on the other hand, is something different, requires more effort, and brings you up again in their memory a couple of days later in a positive way.

DAY 7

How to
Make a Bed

———◆———

83

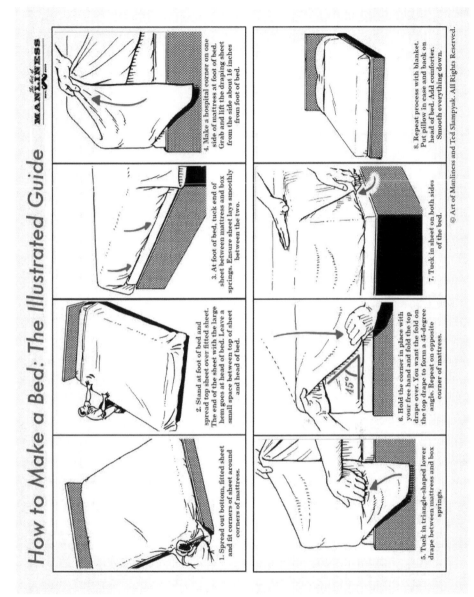

How to Make a Bed: The Illustrated Guide

1. Spread out bottom, fitted sheet and fit corners of sheet around corners of mattress.

2. Stand at foot of bed and spread top sheet over fitted sheet. The end of the sheet with the large hem goes at head of bed. Leave a small space between top of sheet and head of bed.

3. At foot of bed, tuck end of sheet between mattress and box springs. Ensure sheet lays smoothly between the two.

4. Make a hospital corner on one side of mattress at foot of bed. Grab and lift the draping sheet from the side about 16 inches from foot of bed.

5. Tuck in triangle-shaped lower drape between mattress and box springs.

6. Hold the corner in place with your free hand and fold the top drape over. You want the fold on the top drape to form a 45-degree angle. Repeat on opposite corner of mattress.

45°

7. Tuck in sheet on both sides of the bed.

8. Repeat process with blanket. Put pillow in case and back on head of bed. Add comforter. Smooth everything down.

W hy make your bed? Well, not only does doing it every day build your discipline, which strengthens your will-power, keeping your place looking orderly helps conserve your day-to-day willpower supply as well, so you can channel it into more important tasks. Plus it just looks nice, and it feels really good to get into a made bed when you turn in each night.

DAY 8

Living with
Roommates

If you're like most young men leaving the nest for the first time, you probably won't have enough money to live all by yourself. To save money, you'll very likely have to bunk with a roommate or two to cut down on living costs. While roommates can save you money (and provide camaraderie and companionship), they can pose many challenges. Any time you put two people with different backgrounds and lifestyles together under one roof, there's bound to be conflict and awkward social moments.

Learning how to effectively manage the roommate relationship is an essential skill for every young man to have. Not only will it make living with roommates during your bachelor years easier, it also prepares you in many ways for when you settle down and start a family of your own.

Below we provide some tips on how to make living with roommates as drama-free as possible. The advice is based on my personal experience of living with dozens of roommates when I was single, many of whom came from completely different cultures than me.

Establish ground rules from the get-go. A friend of mine who left home a year earlier than me summed up this guideline thusly: *"Establish rules before you need them."* Don't wait until someone forgets to pay their share of the rent to figure out what happens when someone doesn't pay the rent. Neither should you wait until the night before a big final to have the discussion about your roommate's proclivity for blasting his TV at 2am in the morning.

The best thing you can do to get along with your roommate is to sit down with him the first day you move in (if you're in the dorms) or before you sign a lease (if you're getting an apartment) to discuss the rules of the apartment/dorm. Don't make this conversation combative. Don't be defensive and uptight. You want everyone to be as open and frank as possible. You can say something like, "Just so we're on the same page and so we can avoid any conflicts in the future, can we lay down some ground rules for the apartment?"

What sort of rules should you establish? Here's a list of a few questions you might consider bringing up in your conversation with your roommate:

- When should everyone pay their share of the rent and utility bills?
- Who cleans what and when? Also discuss the consequences if people don't do their chores.
- What are the rules on dishes? Do dirty dishes get put in the dishwasher right away or can you leave them in the sink? Who unloads the dishes?
- Is smoking allowed inside?
- What are everyone's drinking habits?
- What sort of expenses will we share? Cleaning supplies? Garbage bags? Toilet paper? Any shared food expenses like coffee and milk?
- What are the rules on bringing guests over? Can friends crash in the living room? How big of a heads-up should everyone give before having a party or bringing guests over? Do we even need to give a heads-up?
- What about significant others? Can they spend the night? Can they hang out all day, every day? Can we give them

duplicates of our keys? You've got to be careful with this one. I've seen several roommate relationships go south because a girlfriend slowly turned into a non-paying third tenant. Nip that in the bud from the get-go.

• Speaking of significant others, if you're sharing a room with a roommate, you might want to establish some sort of "Do Not Disturb" signal. It will save you from some awkward walk-ins.

• What are the rules on morning and nighttime noise levels?

• Are pets allowed?

• What temperature are we going to keep the thermostat set at? (You'd be surprised how contentious this issue can be with roommates.)

• Have everyone share whether they're neat freaks or slobs. It's best to know from the outset so you can manage expectations about what constitutes a clean apartment.

A lot of roommate conflict boils down to a mismatch of expectations. Roommates expect each other to be mind-readers, and to live up to expectations that they've never actually verbalized, but simply expect the other guy to magically know and adhere to. When the expectations aren't met, resentment follows. By sitting down together before you move in, you'll know what to expect. For whatever psychological reason, even when someone doesn't meet your standards, if you already know that they won't, you won't get bent out of shape about it.

By the way, I know some will feel resistant to the idea of drawing up ground rules. You probably feel like you're young and want to keep things loose and that because you're buddies, things will just naturally work out. Maybe they will, maybe they won't. Think of the ground rules as friendship insurance — getting a policy isn't the most pleasant task, and maybe you won't need it, but if you do, it can keep your friendships intact and make the whole experience smoother and more enjoyable.

Be flexible and willing to compromise (but stand firm on your deal-breakers). During your conversation about ground rules, you and your roommates will inevitably run into disagreements. Be flexible and work to compromise in order to accommodate each other's differing lifestyles. For example, if you're a night owl and your roommate is not, you should be willing to keep the noise down after he goes to bed, and he should try to get ready quietly in the morning when you're still snoozing. If there are some things that are deal-breakers for you, don't be afraid to stand your ground. If you don't want any smoking in the house, say so. If your roommate isn't willing to adjust to your request, find a new place or roommate.

Follow the Golden Rule. The key to managing roommate relationships is to be mutually respectful and considerate of one another. You will be well served by following the Golden Rule. If you don't like walking into your living room to unexpectedly find a stranger sacked out on the couch, don't invite friends over without giving your roommate a heads-up; don't touch your roommate's stuff without asking permission first; don't leave your dirty dishes in the common area. You get the idea.

Have a weekly sync-up meeting. One activity that I found immensely useful in managing and preventing roommate conflicts is having a weekly meeting to sync up with each other. At this meeting you can discuss bills that need to be paid and chores that need to be done. It's also a good time to let your roommate know about guests that are coming over in the coming week, so they have a heads-up.

The sync-up meeting is a good time to bring up and resolve any issues that are causing friction between roommates. Again, don't be combative when you bring up concerns. Just tell your roommate what's been bothering you and ask what the two of you can do to resolve the issue.

I'd also use this time to ask my roommate if there's anything I can do to help him out that week. For example, if I knew that he was working overtime to finish a school paper, I'd ask if there were any chores or errands I could help out with that week. My roommates would do the same for me when I was getting bogged down.

Another nice feature about the weekly sync-up meeting is that it carries over nicely to married life. Kate and I do something similar in our own relationship. It's a practice that has definitely contributed to our success in both our marriage and our business.

There will be conflict. Address it calmly and directly instead of avoiding it. Conflict and disagreements are a normal part of any relationship, be it in a marriage or with a roommate. So don't be surprised if you and your roommate don't get along all the time. Unfortunately, many young people handle conflict by simply acting like it doesn't exist or hoping that the conflict will magically resolve itself. Managing conflict like this will only turn small issues into big ones. Don't avoid conflict. Don't leave each other passive aggressive notes. Instead, rip off that band-aid and understand that "pain now is better than pain deferred." So if you notice that your roommate is slacking off on his chores or is ~~stealing~~ borrowing your food, bring it up as soon as you can. Don't let the conflict fester until it blows up like a puss-filled boil.

Understand you don't have to be best friends with your roommate. One mistake I've seen many young people make when entering roommate relationships for the first time is having unreasonably high-expectations about the relationship. They expect that they'll be best buddies with their roommates and do everything together and never get in fights. Their roommate, on the other hand, prefers to have his space and spend time with his own friends. This mismatch in expectations can cause friction in the relationship from the get-go.

To prevent this mismatch of expectations, understand that you and your roommate might not be best buds, but merely roommates who respect each other. While you should certainly invite your roommate out to a party or a ballgame, don't get offended if he declines. That's his prerogative.

Even if you're rooming with your best friend from high school, understand that just because you're good friends doesn't mean you'll naturally be good roommates. I've seen volatile roommate fights between people who were once best friends. The problem usually stems from poor expectation management. Best buds naively assume that they'll get along without establishing ground rules or having weekly sync-up meetings. But they don't. Don't skip those steps if you're moving in with a good friend.

Friendships can also deteriorate if you rely on each other for all your social and emotional needs. Even if you're two manly peas in a pod, don't spend all your time with each other. Make other friends, find different interests, and do things separately sometimes.

Use Google Docs and Google Calendars to manage everything. During my roommate days, the only tool we had to manage shared expenses and chores was a whiteboard. My roommates and I would post rent due dates and the chores list for the week. And of course, the whiteboard was used occasionally for scribbling passive aggressive notes about some grievance.

Take a tip from the blog Apartment Therapy and upgrade from the humble whiteboard to the cloud by using shared Google documents and calendars to manage your roommate experience:

- Create a Google spreadsheet to manage rent and other shared expenses.
- Another spreadsheet can be used to keep track of chores and whether they've been done.
- Create and share a Google Calendar just for your roommates so you keep everyone abreast of when guests are coming over or dates for parties. You can also put rent and utility due dates on the calendar and have Google send everyone an email reminder when the date rolls around.
- Use a shared Google document to share random notes.

If your roomies don't use Google, you'll have to convince them to sign up to take advantage of this system.

GoodMate is a new web app that allows you to manage the roommate experience from a central dashboard. You can manage shared expenses, chores, and calendars all within GoodMate. The service will email your roommates with reminders to pay rent or do their chores. The only downside to GoodMate is that you have to sign-in with Facebook. If you have a roommate who doesn't use Facebook, you'll have to use the whiteboard. And look into whether he hasn't time-traveled to your apartment from the year 2002.

I CAN'T STAND MY ROOMMATE. WHAT CAN I DO?

Despite doing your darnedest to make it work, your relationship with your roommate has reached a point that you can't imagine living another day with him. What can you do?

If you're living in a dorm, go talk to your RA. They might be able to help you make a room switch. I had a friend in college who decided to get assigned a random dorm roommate for the "experience." Little did she know that the roommate assigned to her would turn out to be certifiably crazy. After a few weeks of trying to make the relationship work, my friend asked for a new dorm room. She got one with little trouble.

If you're living in an apartment, getting rid of a bad roommate or moving out is a bit trickier because of the lease agreement. Unless you have enough money to pay for the months remaining in your lease agreement, plus an early termination fee, moving out might not be an option. You could always evict your roommate, but that process can take time and makes an already awkward situation even awkwarder. The eviction process is a bit complex for this book, so you'll have to do some research on your own.

Unless your apartment roommate is not paying their share of the rent or is conducting illegal activities in your apartment, your best bet is to wait until the lease is up and go your separate ways. If nothing else, it will be a learning experience.

DAY 9

Managing Your Online Reputation

—•—

All the basic life skills we've covered so far in this book have been things that your dad, and even your granddad, had to learn when he left home for the first time too.

But today's young man faces a new challenge that pops never encountered: managing his online reputation.

Despite the nascent nature of this skill, I truly believe it's one of the most important things we'll talk about in this book. As the line between the offline and online world gets increasingly blurry, your online reputation *is* your reputation. Before you meet your freshman roommate, before you pick up a date, before you shake the hand of a potential employer…you better believe they've already Googled you, already formed a first, first impression about you, your interests, and what kind of person you are. Thus, if you're not careful and conscious about the content you create online, you can end up shooting yourself in the foot in all areas of your life.

HEADING OUT ON YOUR OWN…AND INTO A FISHBOWL WORLD

Leaving for college or another kind of adventure after high school has long been an exciting and heady time. It's an age where you're experimenting with ideas and values, testing new freedoms, meeting new people, and often changing your mind about who you are and what you want out of life. One week you feel one way, and the next you feel another. During this process you often make mistakes, and do bone-headed things that twenty years later will still make you wonder, "What was I thinking?"

Just a decade ago, only you and a few of your closest friends would have held the memory of those crazy and sometimes cringe-worthy moments. The only record of them could be found by digging up a private photo album or journal.

Today...it's a whole new ball game.

Now, everything you do and say can potentially become part of your permanent and public record. Everybody's got a smartphone and can snap a picture of you anywhere, anytime, and post it online. And things that go up online about you and from you can remain there forever. Mistakes you made when you were just 19 can haunt you for the rest of your life. Being a young man used to mean you could entirely reinvent yourself by moving to a new place and making new friends, but now your online reputation will follow you wherever you go.

I don't mean to sound all doom and gloom about it, but that's the sobering reality of living in the Internet Age, and it doesn't help to bury one's head in the sand and try to "whatever" that reality away. It absolutely doesn't mean that college can't still be the fun, spontaneous experience it's always been; it just means you need to take a conscious, proactive approach to taking responsibility for what parts of that experience end up online and in the public eye.

WHY IS PROACTIVELY MANAGING YOUR ONLINE REPUTATION SO IMPORTANT?

One of the greatest things about the internet is that it is a giant pot that people can both add to and take from. It puts the most enormous wealth of knowledge in human history right at our fingertips and provides an endless amount of inspiration that can be added onto and "remixed."

The downside of the big internet pot is that the moment you put something into it, you pretty much lose all control over it. Many viral embarrassments have started out as something someone just wanted to share with a few good friends. But those friends shared it with their friends, who shared it with their friends…on and on until it ended up on *Tosh.O*.

There are essentially no guaranteed take backs when it comes to what you put online. You can erase your Facebook status, blog post, comment, tweet, or video, but someone else may very well have already shared it, copied it, taken a screenshot of it, or downloaded the video and reposted it somewhere else. How websites looked on a certain date in time are captured and archived on sites like the Wayback Machine. Emails that you thought you deleted forever can still sometimes be retrieved, and just because you deleted an email doesn't mean the person you sent it to didn't archive it. If someone else wants to post something of yours, you may not be able to get them to take it down without suing.

All of which is to say, pretty much every piece of digital content you create can potentially exist forever. And this digital record can be accessed by any of the 250 million internet users in the US, not to mention the 2 billion online all over the world.

What's on that record can have a big impact on both your personal and professional life.

Your college's admissions office may have Googled you when they looked over your application. As soon as your freshman roommate knew you'd be bunking with him, he Googled you. When you network with someone at a party and tell them about your great idea, they'll Google you later. And 81% of singles say they Google or check the Facebook page of someone before meeting him or her for a date.

Even though only 7% of Americans think their online reputation influences hiring decisions, in reality, 75% of US companies have made online screening a formal part of the hiring process. 85% of recruiters and HR professionals say that having a positive online reputation influences their hiring decisions, and 70% of recruiters say they have rejected candidates based on something they found about them online. And since those numbers come from a study done in 2009, they're undoubtedly much higher now.

What kinds of online discoveries cause recruiters and HR personnel to push your resume to the trash? This chart shows the most common red flags employers look for:

Types of Online Reputational Information That Influenced Decisions to Reject a Candidate				
	U.S.	U.K.	Germany	France
Concerns about the candidate's lifestyle	58%	45%	42%	32%
Inappropriate comments and text written by the candidate	56%	57%	78%	58%
Unsuitable photos , videos, and information	55%	51%	44%	42%
Inappropriate comments or text written by friends and relatives	43%	35%	14%	11%
Comments criticizing previous employers, co-workers, or clients	40%	40%	28%	37%
Inappropriate comments or text written by colleagues or work acquaintances	40%	37%	17%	21%
Membership in certain groups and networks	35%	33%	36%	37%
Discovered that information the candidate shared was false	30%	36%	42%	47%
Poor communication skills displayed online	27%	41%	17%	42%
Concern about the candidate's financial background	16%	18%	11%	0%

Some young folks may be tempted to respond by saying, "Well, if a company is going to reject me for posting pictures of my drunken revelry, I wouldn't want to work for them anyway." But that's pretty short-sighted. I'd venture to say that these companies aren't rejecting candidates so much because they like to drink or swear, but rather that their willingness to show off these behaviors publicly shows a lack of judgment and wisdom. Not at all an unreasonable assumption.

The information that new friends and potential employers can find about you online may not even be true. Some people will try to verify it, some will not. And what they see will often come without any context – maybe you were being funny, maybe it's an inside joke, etc., but they won't know that, they'll simply make immediate judgments about what they find. This is why when it comes to managing your online reputation, you must be both proactive and defensive — deleting anything inappropriate, wisely choosing the digital content you create, and purposefully creating positive content about yourself.

SELF-REFLECT BEFORE YOU SELF-REVEAL

"Young people in particular often self-reveal before they self-reflect. There is no eraser button today for youthful indiscretion."
—James Steyer

There are some practical ways to manage your online reputation, and we'll get to them in a moment. But the first step in taking responsibility for your online presence is creating a mindset for how you want to approach your online life.

Matt Ivester, the author of *lol...OMG!* (despite the silly-sounding title, this is actually a great book, with solid advice from the guy who learned about online reputation management firsthand from his misadventures in founding Juicycampus. com), suggests three questions to ask yourself before you put something online:

1. WHY ARE YOU DOING THIS?

Why? This is the most important question of all, and one that unfortunately usually goes unasked and uncontemplated.

Today's colleges are welcoming the first "digital natives": they've never known a time when the internet wasn't a huge part of their lives. And even for those who are old enough to have used encyclopedias for elementary-school research papers, interacting and participating online has become so ubiquitous that it's hard to imagine that life was ever any other way. This is just how things are, and we do what everyone else is doing, so much so that we hardly ever ask why we are doing those things. Once we do start asking why, the answers are surprisingly hard to come up with and articulate.

Why do you update your status or share a link on Facebook? Do you want to share news? Are you bored? Do you want to be thought clever? Are you trying to make someone else jealous? Do you want to see if people feel the same way as you? Why?

Why do you care how many likes or upvotes something you submit on Facebook or Reddit gets? Is it confirmation that you shared something with value? Why?

Why do you leave comments on blog posts? Do you want

the author of the blog to know that you appreciated the article? Do you think you have an insight to add that might help another reader? Do you want the author to know how and why they are wrong? Why? What do you hope to accomplish? Do you think it will change their mind? Is it because the psychological angst you feel when you think someone is wrong needs to be discharged? Why?

Why do you participate in online forums? Does it provide a feeling of camaraderie? Do you like to hear others' opinions? Why do you respond when you think those opinions are wrong? Why do you care what a stranger thinks about you? Why?

When you ponder the why behind creating any kind of online content, from a status update to a YouTube video, you may come up with a reason that you find satisfactory and worthwhile. Or you may find that your motivation is hard to make sense of and decide it's not worth your time. Either way, by asking why, you'll become what Ivester calls "a conscious creator of content."

2. IS NOW THE RIGHT TIME?

The internet creates a perfect storm for impulse control: at the same time that it actively solicits impulsive communication and makes satisfying those impulses incredibly easy, it makes taking back the results of those impulses incredibly difficult; it's easy to hit "send" or "submit," and quite hard to un-send and un-submit something.

Facebook asks, "What's on your mind?" and more recently, "How are you feeling?" while Twitter wants to know, "What's happening?" They owe their existence to people's desire to share their thoughts, videos, and photographs – and they need to be constantly fed to survive and grow and make money. And blogs (including ours) want to engage readers and build community and so ask for comments. The internet is set up to encourage you to share whatever thought crosses your mind, and taking that thought from your cranium to the walls and screens of the digital world only takes a few clicks.

But just because you can share your thoughts on impulse doesn't mean you should. Not only because you probably haven't thought through the why behind wanting to share first, but because strong impulses are usually born from strong emotions: anger, depression, and grief, or from chemically-altered states (like being drunk). When you spout off and share personal feelings while emotional or trashed, you will likely come to regret it once those strong emotions fade or you sober up.

The best thing to do when you feel you're dealing with an impulse to put something online that you might regret later is just to sit on it. The internet creates a false sense of imme-diacy, giving you an overwhelming feeling that you have to respond now. But what you'll find is that something that felt super urgent and mega-important to say in the moment will seem totally pointless when you wake up the next morning.

One method I use to thwart impulsive responses is to imag-ine myself living before the internet. If I feel a burning urge to tell the author of an article what a chucklehead he is, I think of reading a magazine in the 80s, and how I would have had no outlet to express my opinion about it besides writing up a letter to the editor or talking to my wife or close friends about it. Or if something annoys me and I want to rant about it on Facebook,

I think of a time before Facebook when I would have had no choice but to keep my rant to myself. It makes me realize that just as sharing whatever crosses your mind wasn't necessary then, it's not necessary now. The fine folks of the 80s, while they made some questionable fashion choices, weren't any less happy than we are now that we're able to shout what we're feeling and thinking to everyone 24/7.

3. HOW CONTROVERSIAL DO YOU WANT TO BE?

The younger generation (including those my age) was raised with a lot of rhetoric about how special and unique they are, how important it is to be "authentic," and that it's good to be "transparent." This can lead folks to throw caution to the wind about what they share online because, "I'm just trying to be me! And if other people don't like it, they can bite me!"

But just because you can now display your opinions and personality to a greater number of people than ever before, doesn't mean you should, or that the more you share, the more authentic you are. Going back to my suggestion of thinking about life before the internet, people used to only be able to share their quirks with a close circle of family and friends, and they weren't any less themselves than we are (actually they were probably more themselves since they didn't get instant feedback on all of their quirks).

Examining the meaning of authenticity isn't within the purview of this chapter (although it will be a future series on the blog), but suffice it to say for now that the ideal for many of the great men of the past was not transparency, but sprezzatura – only revealing themselves to others slowly as a relationship of trust developed. You may want to "be yourself" by trumpeting your religious, social, and political beliefs online every chance you get, but if those memes you keep flooding Facebook with are the only thing new acquaintances know about you, they may decide they don't want to get to know you before they even do — they'll miss the complexity of your character that would have shown through over time…that you're both a liberal and a rabid gun owner, or a fervent Christian and a scientist, or a zealous vegetarian and a Marine.

The three questions above can go a long way to helping you judiciously choose what and what not to post online. A final question to consider is what the general public might think of the content if for some reason what you post went viral or you were suddenly thrust into national prominence. Would it embarrass your family? What impression would a stranger have of it? You and your friends might think it's funny, but would others find it offensive? You never know who's going to see your post, what's going to be dug up on you later, or who might be looking at your phone.

How to Manage Your Online Reputation

Managing your online reputation involves both deleting content you don't want out there and creating content you do. Follow the steps below that Ivester and others have suggested, and complete each step right after you read it. This is the kind of thing that's easy to put off indefinitely. Do it now.

1. Google yourself.

Before you can know what actions to take to manage your online reputation, you need to know what's already out there. To do this, first deactivate Google's customized search – when you typically do a Google search, the results Google brings up are based on things like your location, what you've clicked on before, and things your friends like. But you want to see what would come up if someone else searched for you. To do this, you can sign out of your Google account and re-search.

If you have a common name like "Rob Smith," then search for your name with a qualifier, like "Rob Smith St. Louis," or "Rob Smith Tulane University."

After you look at Google's results for you, check out other search engines like Bing and Yahoo as well.

When you look at the results that come up for your name, try to imagine what conclusions someone might reach about you if they had no other context for that content, and knew nothing else about you.

2. TRY TO REMOVE CONTENT THAT YOU DON'T WANT SHOWING UP IN SEARCH RESULTS ANYMORE.

After you do a search for yourself, it's time to try to delete things that showed up that you'd rather not have out there anymore. Maybe you signed up for an internet forum with your real name. Maybe you left a comment on a blog post under your real name. Maybe you wrote a review or a blog post that you now feel is too controversial. Some of these things you can delete yourself.

If you can't delete something yourself, like a blog post

comment on another person's blog, then try to contact the owner of the site to see if they will remove it for you. They may or may not, but the nicer you are about it, the greater the chance of them helping you, so make your request as civil and appreciative as possible.

If you can't find the contact information for the site owner, try the site WHOis. Website registrars are required to publish the contact information for the person who registered the domain. Oftentimes when you look up a site on WHOis.com, you'll find that the owner has decided to keep their direct contact information private and have instead given a proxy email address. Either way, your email will end up in the same place.

Understand that even if you're successful at removing the offending content from a site, it may take a few days or even weeks before it's reflected in search engine results. Also, understand that the offending item really hasn't "gone away." There's a chance that it has been archived on the Wayback Machine. Remember, what's put on the internet stays on the internet forever.

Moving forward, be extremely judicious when using your real name online.

3. PROACTIVELY CREATE A POSITIVE FIRST IMPRESSION ONLINE.

Your best bet in managing your online reputation is proactively creating positive content about yourself that pushes the bad stuff off of the first few pages of search engines. Set up accounts with large social networking sites that typically rank high on Google and other search engines. Twitter, LinkedIn, Facebook, and Google+ profiles are often on the first page when you look up someone's name. Set up accounts with them and post stuff that you'd be proud to have your name associated with.

The best thing you can do to ensure positive stuff associated with your name is at the top of search results is to start a blog and update it regularly. If you can, try to secure a domain name with your given name for your blog. What should you write about on your blog? You can publish your resume (redacting phone numbers and addresses, of course), write posts sharing insights in an expertise you might have, or use it to create a portfolio of your work if you're a freelancer. Whatever it is, make sure it's stuff you want associated with your name.

Cross-link your blog and all your social networking profiles together: put your link to Facebook and Twitter on your blog, a link to your LinkedIn profile and blog on your Facebook account, and so on.

Even if you don't plan on using Twitter or Google+ or even putting anything on your blog, it doesn't hurt to have your name registered with those accounts and domain. You don't want some Joe Schmo mucking up your good name with a bunch of crazy online antics.

4. ADJUST PRIVACY SETTINGS ON FACEBOOK AND CLEAN UP YOUR FACEBOOK PROFILE.

To ensure that potential employers or love interests only see the best of you when they look you up on Facebook, make the following adjustments:

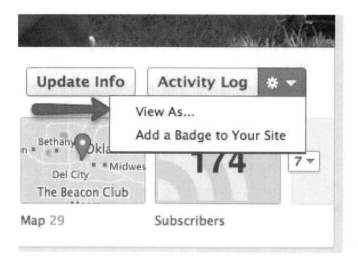

First, take a look at how your profile page looks to the public. If you see any information visible that you don't want strangers to see, make a note of it.

To change what's visible on your profile page, click "About."

Click "Edit" on the next page. On each segment select "Friends" if you don't want anybody who's not your FB friend to see a particular piece of information. For networking reasons, I've left my job and school information visible to the public.

Visit the Facebook Privacy Settings webpage and adjust all your privacy settings so only your friends can see photos and status updates you make.

On the privacy settings page, update what your friends can share about you under "Timeline and Tagging." Enable the ability to review and approve posts or photos that you are tagged in before they're published on your Timeline. You can also disable Facebook's tag suggestion when your friends upload photos that look like you. You don't want your name tagged in an unflattering photo or post.

While you're on the privacy settings page, limit who can see posts from the past. Even if you used to post everything publicly, this will retroactively make those posts private.

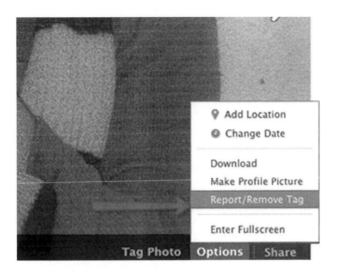

Review the photos that you're tagged in and untag yourself from any unflattering photos. While you're at it, you might ask your friend to remove the photo if it's something you don't want out there. Even if you're not tagged in the pic, it could come back to haunt you.

5. BE MORE CONSCIOUS OF WHAT YOU SHARE AND WHOM YOU SHARE IT WITH ON FACEBOOK.

Ask the three questions we covered above before posting something on Facebook. That will save you a lot of grief.

Also, take into account if what you're about to share is appropriate and relevant to ALL your Facebook friends. You don't need to share your weekend plans with your old boss and former professors. In real life, you adjust what you talk about depending on your company — do the same on Facebook. Create lists on Facebook for close family/friends, acquaintances, professional colleagues, people that are the same religion as you, people you enjoy talking politics with, etc. Before posting something, ask yourself if this is something all your friends would be interested in or if it is better for a specific list of your friends. And even if you're only posting for a list of close friends, still keep in mind what others would think if that status or photo got shared with people outside the list. It could happen.

6. CREATE STRONG PASSWORDS FOR YOUR ACCOUNTS.

If the recent story of tech writer Mat Honan's online life being completely demolished by hackers (can be found at *honan.net*) doesn't motivate you to strengthen your online security, then I don't know what will. Create strong passwords for all your accounts and change them every six months. A strong password is at least 8 characters long and includes at least one special character (&!#) and both upper and lower case letters. Your passwords shouldn't be the same for all your accounts. To manage all your passwords, use an app like LastPass.

To reduce the chance of getting hacked, enable two-step authentication. You can easily Google how to do this for both Gmail and Facebook.

7. USE PASSWORDS ON YOUR LAPTOP AND MOBILE DEVICES.

An unattended laptop or mobile device provides a devilish opportunity for friends or random strangers to mess with your online life. I know several people who had to do a lot of scrambling to recover from an offensive tweet sent from an unattended iPhone by a mischievous friend. Avoid that. Enable password protection on all your mobile devices.

8. SET UP A GOOGLE ALERT FOR YOUR NAME.

Keep your finger on the pulse of what's said about you on the web by setting up a Google Alert for your name. Just enter your name as a search query and Google Alerts will email you a digest once a week (or daily if you want) of all the new content that's hit the web with your name in it.

CONCLUSION

The internet is an amazing educational, social, and networking tool — you just need to use it wisely. Using it too little can be just as damaging to your personal and professional life as using it too much. Be a "conscious content creator" and use sound wisdom and judgment in deciding where you personally want to draw the line between your public and private life.

DAY 10

How to Tie the
Half-Windsor
Necktie Knot

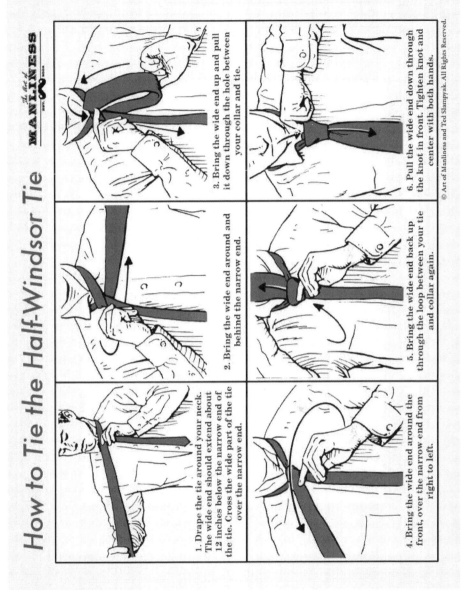

How to Tie the Half-Windsor Tie

1. Drape the tie around your neck. The wide end should extend about 12 inches below the narrow end of the tie. Cross the wide part of the tie over the narrow end.

2. Bring the wide end around and behind the narrow end.

3. Bring the wide end up and pull it down through the hole between your collar and tie.

4. Bring the wide end and around the front, over the narrow end from right to left.

5. Bring the wide end back up through the loop between your tie and collar again.

6. Pull the wide end down through the knot in front. Tighten knot and center with both hands.

Many young men heading out on their own for the first time have never tied a tie themselves. If that's you, I'd recommend the Half-Windsor as the first necktie knot you learn.

While the Four-in-Hand is the easiest knot to tie, the Half-Windsor looks more symmetrical and formal, while being less bulky than the Full Windsor. It's a very versatile knot, appropriate for all occasions, and goes well with nearly every collar type, except narrow collars.

Once you've mastered the Half-Windsor, branch out and learn how to tie other necktie knots, and the bowtie as well.

DAY 11

Understand
Credit

125

*C*redit. When it comes to understanding personal finance, this component looms large. For some it is a dirty word, to be avoided at all costs. For others, it is an intoxicating license, an opportunity to reach for a lifestyle well beyond their means.

In truth, credit can be either extremely helpful or extremely harmful depending on how it's used. In many ways, credit is more of a tool than anything else – simply a means of achieving some desired outcome. In the hands of an uneducated, unskilled, and inexperienced person, a fire, a table saw, or a gun can cause havoc and harm. But in the hands of a responsible and educated individual, they can be immensely useful. So it is with credit.

A bad use of credit would be buying a huge flatscreen television with a credit card; you'll receive little return on the interest you'll pay on that balance. A good use of credit would be taking out loans to get an education, or for a car to get you to and from a job; these things put you in debt in the short-term, but will improve your financial prospects in the long-term.

When you need to use credit in a positive way, your ability to do so will be based on the credit history and score you have been establishing for years, starting when you first headed out on your own.

WHAT IS CREDIT?

As the dictionary defines it, credit is: "The ability to obtain goods or services before payment, based on the trust that payment will be made in the future." Student loans, car loans, home mortgages, and credit cards are all types of consumer credit instruments — you're getting money *now* to pay for something you otherwise couldn't afford, based on the lender trusting that you'll pay them back *later*.

Sometimes credit is completely free, but it usually comes at a price. Most banks and institutions will charge *interest* on the money they lend you (aka, the principle) in exchange for giving you the funds, along with the opportunity to pay it back slowly over an extended period of time.

Different types of credit have different interest rates. Student loans often have lower interest rates than other types because many of them are guaranteed by the U.S. government. Even if you can't pay them back, the lender will still get their money from the government. Credit cards, on the other hand, often have the highest interest rates among the various types of credit because: 1) there's a higher risk that the credit card lender won't get repaid and 2) it's more expensive to manage credit card debt (at least that's what the credit card companies say).

Even among the same kinds of loans, you'll find different interest rates. That's because people have varying degrees of "creditworthiness." You'll often hear banks refer to people as having "good credit," "bad credit," or "no credit." People with good credit have a reputation for being a responsible borrower. They pay their bills on time and manage the credit available to them responsibly. People with good credit not only have access to more money, they also get lower interest rates on their loans.

People with bad credit have a reputation for not paying their bills on time or even not paying them at all. Banks and other businesses are less willing to extend credit to these individuals.

Even if they're able to get a loan, a person with bad credit will be charged a higher interest rate.

Folks with no credit simply don't have a history of using credit, so they're kind of a wild card. They might be good with credit, or they might not. When banks loan money to people in this situation, they'll usually start off charging a higher interest rate, but they'll be willing to bring it down as the debtor demonstrates they can repay the balance owed on a consistent basis.

How Do Banks Know If You're Creditworthy?

So how do banks or credit card companies know whether you have good credit, bad credit, or no credit? When you apply for a loan, the person reviewing the application probably doesn't know you from Adam. How can they possibly discern whether or not they can trust you to pay them back?

Put on your tin foil hat folks, because the answer is that there are three big credit agencies keeping track of how you use credit — from how much you borrow to how often you are late on payments.

You've probably seen the commercials on TV about how to get your hands on a *free credit report*. That's the record those Big Brother-like agencies have on you. These commercials will also typically mention something called a *credit score*. That's the number that banks use to indicate whether you're a trustworthy borrower or not.

Many young people just getting their feet wet in the world of credit often confuse credit reports with credit scores, and vice versa. It's an easy mistake to make, but one that can be corrected with a quick primer on the difference between the two.

What's a Credit Report?

Credit reports explain what you do with your credit. They state when and where you applied for credit, whom you borrowed money from, and whom you still owe. Your credit report also tells if you've paid off a debt and if you make monthly payments on time.

Federal law mandates that all three major credit reporting agencies must each give you a free credit report each year. So, when those TV commercials talk about getting a free credit report, the above information is what they're offering.

But, getting your free credit report from a heavily-advertised site like FreeCreditReport.com or FreeCreditScore.com isn't a good idea. In return for getting a free credit report and score, you have to enroll in their monthly credit-monitoring service for $15 a month. If you cancel within seven days, the report and score are indeed free, but if not, your subscription to their service will begin. The pain is that you have to call to cancel — you can't do it online — and you might forget (that's what they're counting on).

Instead, get your free credit report with no strings attached from AnnualCreditReport.com. This site offers you a truly free report from each of the three credit agencies. You can get them all at once, but I would recommend staggering them throughout the year so you can keep more regular tabs on your credit report.

Why You Need to Request Your Credit Report Every Year

There are a couple of reasons why you should request a free

credit report each year. First, it allows you to check for and correct mistakes that have crept into your report. You don't want those mistakes to affect whether you get a higher or lower interest rate, or whether a bank will approve a loan for you at all. When you spot a mistake, you can start taking actions to clean it up.

The second big reason you want to request a credit report every year is to protect yourself from identity theft. With the right information, a con artist can apply for a wallet full of credit cards in your name without you knowing it. Then you start getting calls out of the blue from collection agencies asking you to pay up on purchases you never made. A yearly credit report lets you check to see if anybody is fraudulently using your name to apply for credit cards or loans without your knowledge and you can take action if needed.

WHAT'S A CREDIT SCORE?

Your credit score is determined by the information in your credit report. Credit scores are used by companies and banks to evaluate the potential risk posed by lending money to individual consumers. Your credit score determines if you qualify for a loan, what your loan's interest rate will be, and what your credit limit is. It's basically your trustworthiness score for lenders.

The company that came up with the idea of a credit score was the Fair Isaac Corporation (FICO). That's why you've probably heard credit scores referred to as a FICO score. Because each of the three credit agencies collects slightly different information about you, you'll have three different credit scores, although it's possible for all of them to be the same.

Credit scores range from 500 to 850, with higher scores being better. If you have a FICO score of 500, you're going to have a hard time getting a loan. Even if you manage to get one, the interest rate on it will be high. With any score above 720, you'll receive the best rates available. Whenever you apply for a credit card or car loan, banks and credit card companies will check your score to determine whether to lend you money or extend the credit card to you in the first place. If they do decide to extend you credit, they'll then use your credit score to determine the interest rate they'll charge.

Unlike credit reports, which are free, credit scores cost money to view. They cost about $15 to access, and you're given the offer to purchase your credit score after you get a credit report. Bankrate.com, however, offers a free FICO score estimator. The estimator asks you 10 questions about your loans and credit card balances and then spits out an estimate of your credit score. While not 100% accurate, you'll at least have an idea of where your score is at and make adjustments in order to improve it.

HOW YOUR CREDIT SCORE IS DETERMINED

Because your credit score can possibly make or break some important financial and lifestyle decisions, it's important to understand how the credit agencies determine your score so you can take actions to ensure it's the best it can be.

When coming up with your FICO score, credit reporting companies look at several factors, including:

Payment record. 35% of your score depends on your ability to pay your bills on time. Payments that are more than 90 days late will hurt more than a payment that's just 30 days late. Also, recent late payments hurt more than older ones. A single late payment won't kill your score, so don't panic that you'll never be creditworthy because you missed a payment. Just pay the bill and try not to let it happen again.

Amount borrowed relative to available credit. This factor accounts for 30% of your score. The credit companies want to know if you're borrowing to the max. If you have $10,000 of available credit, and you consistently run a balance of $9,999, that's a red flag that you're not very prudent about your debt. However, if you usually have a balance of $200 of outstanding debt, that's a sign you're more responsible. To improve your score, try to keep your debt to about 10% or less of your available credit.

Length of credit history. This is 15% of your score. The longer you have successfully borrowed money and paid it back, the less risk you are to a lender. If you pay off a credit card, it's good to keep it open, even if you never use it. When you close it, you lose that credit history, which could affect your score.

"Hard" credit pulls. This is 10% of your credit score. A pull is a type of inquiry into your credit. Hard credit inquiries are made by lenders for the purpose of extending you credit. These will lower your score because having multiple hard inquiries is a signal that you're looking for loans and are possibly a poor credit risk. So, when the cashier asks if you want to sign-up for a store credit card to get a 10% discount, tell them "no thanks" in order to avoid the hard credit pull.

If you're shopping around for a car loan or mortgage, lenders will have to pull your credit score every time you ask for a quote. Don't worry about those types of pulls hurting your score. Similar inquiries made within a two-week period won't ding you.

Types of debt. This is the final 10% of your score. It's best to have a mix of car, home, student loans, and little to no credit card debt. If you're up to your eyeballs in credit card debt, you'll be seen as bigger risk.

Other factors. In addition to your FICO score, lenders will also to take into account other factors when determining whether to loan you money. Things like your income, job history, and assets (money in the bank, car, home, etc. – basically, your earthly possessions) you own can factor into whether you can secure a loan.

HOW CAN I BUILD AND IMPROVE MY CREDIT HISTORY AND SCORE?

Because your payment record and length of credit history make up about 50% of your credit score, it's important you begin building a solid credit history as soon as you can. A good credit history along with a high credit score will serve you well later in life.

The fastest and surest way to build up your credit history

is to simply open up credit accounts and pay back the money when it's due. Opening a credit card account is an easy way for young people to begin establishing their credit history. A low interest, low minimum balance credit card can give a young person just starting out in life the opportunity to pay a credit balance on a regular basis in order to establish a solid positive payment record. Also, the earlier a young person obtains a credit card, the longer his credit history will be when he applies for that mortgage later in life.

There is a danger, though. Credit cards can be a big-time hazard for a young man just starting out on his own, as they allow you to spend money you don't have. And because a young man's schedule can be hectic and his life disorganized, he may forget to pay the monthly balance, incurring penalties and interest, and potentially plunging him into debt. **If you don't have the income and level of responsibility to pay off your credit card balance every single month, don't get a credit card.**

Even if you are responsible enough to get a credit card, maybe you just don't like the idea of having one and want to avoid credit card debt altogether during your younger years. Smart move.

So what if, for whatever reason, you want to avoid getting a credit card; is there any way to still build up your credit history or are you doomed to high interest rates when you apply for a mortgage later on?

Despite what some people may tell you, **it *is* possible to establish a credit history and improve your credit score without a credit card.** If you're a college student, you likely have student loans. As soon as you graduate, start paying your loans back on a consistent basis. Boom. You've got a credit history.

Another way to establish your history without a credit card is to apply for a small loan through your bank and have your parents co-sign on it. Make regular payments and pay it off as fast as you can. More credit history.

But let's say you're a complete Dave Ramsey devotee and decide to not use credit at all: no credit cards, no student loans, no car loans. Nothing. How can you secure a low interest rate when you're ready to buy a house if you don't have any credit history (assuming you haven't reached the Ramsey pinnacle and are able to buy a house in full with cash!)?

By applying for a PRBC Alternative Credit Score. A PRBC Credit Score shows lenders you're financially responsible and trustworthy by keeping track of how well you pay non-credit bills like rent, utilities, and insurance on a regular basis. It's relatively new, but many lenders will accept a PRBC Alternative Credit Score when determining interest rates for mortgages and other loans. Unlike your traditional credit history or scores that begin tallying as soon as you use credit, you'll need to self-enroll to obtain a PRBC Alternative Credit Score.

DAY 12

What to Do
if You Get in
a Car Accident

———◆———

Getting in a car accident is no fun. I can still remember my first (and only!) accident. It happened just a few weeks after I turned 16. Rear-ended a guy. My small, but noble, Isuzu Hombre was no match for the other guy's giant Ford F-150. The front end of my comparatively small pick-up was swallowed underneath the rear bumper of the truck I hit. While he had just a few dings, my vehicle was totaled.

I remember getting out of my truck feeling sort of shell-shocked. I made sure the other person was okay and was relieved to find out that I hadn't maimed or injured anyone. By then, my friends who had been driving behind me arrived at the scene of the crash. They tried to console me, but all I did was pace back and forth, pointing at my car and yelling, "MY CAR IS SCREWED!" over and over again like a crazy man. Not my finest moment. My friends thought it was the funniest thing in the world, however, and still rib me about it.

I had no clue what I was supposed to do in a car accident, but I knew someone who did: dear old Mom. I called my mom on my 1999 Motorola MicroTac (eat your heart out Zach Morris), and she was on the scene in no time flat, ready to basically take care of things for me.

But what would have happened if I had gotten in the accident when I was a few years older and hundreds of miles away from home at college? Would I have known how to handle the situation correctly without Mom and Dad? Probably not.

To avoid pulling a Brett and going crazy when you get in an accident, read this article and prepare yourself.

Note: This advice applies to accidents when it is obvious you or someone else are not seriously injured. If you are, call 911 immediately, or if you cannot, hope that someone else will, and wait for the ambulance to arrive.

Stay calm. Now is not the time to lose your cool. Keep your wits about yourself.

Safety is your top priority. Your first priority is to maintain the safety of everyone involved in the accident and to take actions to prevent more smash-ups and injuries. If the accident is minor and the cars are still functioning, move them off or to the side of the road.

If the cars aren't going anywhere without a tow truck, turn on your hazard lights, exit the vehicle when it's safe to do so, and walk to the side of the road and out of traffic. Ideally, you should have a warning triangle or flares in your car's emergency kit. Place those on the road to give other drivers a heads-up on the accident. You don't want another car plowing into your pile-up.

Check for injuries. Ask everyone who was in the car with you if they're okay. Then check on the driver and passengers of the other car. Call 911 for an ambulance if needed.

Call the police. After an accident, the other person involved might suggest not calling the police and settling things between just the two of you. Ignore him and call the police, even if it's just a minor fender bender. Here's why:

By law, you may be required to call the police. In most states, you're only required to call the authorities after a car accident if someone has been injured, the accident is blocking traffic, or property damage (including cars) is above a certain monetary amount. Failure to comply with the law could result in an additional fine, so don't try to judge for yourself if those requirements have been met. Let the police dispatcher decide that. After you've described the accident to the dispatch, they may or may not decide to send officers to the scene. If they don't, they'll usually tell you to file an accident report at a station or online.

A police report can help establish liability. The insurance companies of the respective drivers will work together to determine fault. One of the most credible documents the insurers will use in doing so is an official police report. Without a report, figuring out liability becomes an issue of he said/she said. If you were the one hit, you definitely want a police report. I know a few instances where people didn't call the police after an accident, and ultimately regretted not doing so. Those involved exchanged information, but when the drivers who were hit called the offending drivers' insurance companies to make a claim, the offending drivers denied the whole thing and accused the victim of insurance fraud. That wouldn't have happened with a police report.

Even if you are responsible for the accident, you should still call the police. It could be the case that the driver you hit contributed to the accident and shares responsibility, or there may have been factors beyond your control that reduce your responsibility. If you don't want to be held completely liable for the accident and have your insurance rates jacked up, get that information in an official police report.

Even if the police don't come, file a report as soon as you can. At least you'll have your side of the story on record. That can help in the insurance claim.

A police report can protect you from fraud. You come to a red light and roll to a stop behind a car. The light turns green and as the car in front of you begins driving forward, so do you. All of sudden, the car in front of you immediately stops, causing you to rear-end the other driver. While it's certainly possible the driver in front of you had a good reason to stop, it's also possible that he's a fraudster pulling the old "start-and-stop" auto-insurance scam on you.

Individuals who stage accidents in order to fraudulently collect insurance money will often suggest not calling the police and just exchanging information. But even if the accident is minor, call the police. Officers are trained at detecting staged accidents. Having them at the scene can help expose the fraud so you're not held liable for what happened.

Having the police on the scene can keep everyone calm and collected. Emotions can run high at an accident.

Having the police there to act as an impartial referee can ensure that things don't get too heated.

Bottom line: call the police no matter what. If the accident is a minor one, don't call 911, just call the non-emergency number for the local department (you might want to program this number into your phone).

Before the officer leaves, get his name and badge number.

Exchange information with the other driver. You'll want to exchange the following information with the other driver:

- Name
- Address
- Telephone number
- Email
- Driver's license number and state
- Insurance company
- Policy number

You don't need a Social Security number in order to file a police report or claim. If a driver or even the police ask for it, politely, but firmly say, "You don't need that information in order to file a claim/report."

You should always have a pen and notebook in your car, so you can write down the details we mention above and below. Alternatively, many insurance companies now offer extremely useful apps that not only allow you to record the details of the accident, but also have features which help you "draw" the scene of the accident, take photos, collect witness observations, jot down notes, and even file the claim.

Write down the information about the car accident. After you've exchanged information with the other driver, write down the following information about the accident itself:

- Time
- Location of accident (it also doesn't hurt to draw a rough sketch of how you think the accident went down)
- Description of other car, including: make, model, year, color, license plate number, and any visible damage
- Description of individuals involved in accident, including passengers

Take plenty of pictures. Use the camera on your cellphone to document the vehicle damage. The more pictures the better. Keep in mind that you want your photos to show the overall context of the accident so that you can make your case to a claims adjuster. Take pictures from a distance to show the accident in its entirety, as well as pictures up close to show property damage. If there are any skid marks, take pictures of those too. If you think you were responsible for the accident, take pictures of the car you hit from the rear, front, and sides. That way, if the driver accuses you of causing damage to his car that existed prior to the accident, you'll be able to prove he's lying.

Get witness information. If there are witnesses, try to get their information, including their name, address, and phone number. Their observations can help your case in assigning liability.

Don't admit fault or assign blame. Even if it's obvious

whose fault the accident was, don't ever admit fault or assign blame. That's for the police and insurance companies to figure out. While it may pain your inner-gentleman to do so, don't say, "I'm sorry." It's an admission of fault. As soon as you exchange information with the driver and find out he or she is okay, zip your lip and keep discussion to a minimum. You don't want to say anything that could be used against you during the insurance claims process or police report. The only people you want to talk to about the accident are the police and your insurance company.

Call your insurance company. Regardless of fault, call your insurance company and report the accident as soon as possible. If it is your fault, your policy likely requires that you do so. Calling your insurer to report the accident also ensures you get your side of the story on record before the other driver files a claim. That can put you at an advantage in reducing the amount the other driver claims.

If the accident is the other driver's fault, you have the option to call their insurance company and file a claim on your own without even letting your own company know about the accident. But it's probably better that your insurance company files the claim on your behalf. The other driver's insurer is going to do whatever it can to give you the least amount of money. Instead of trying to fight a giant corporation for the money you deserve, let another giant corporation (your insurance company) do the fighting for you.

When you call the insurance company, give them your information, when and where the accident occurred, and the insurance information of the other driver. If the other driver didn't have insurance, give the driver's name and address. Let the agent know that a police report has been filed and that you took pictures.

Your insurance company will send out an adjuster to look at your car and give you an estimate on the damage. The other driver's company will also send out their own adjuster to get their estimate. The two insurance companies will duke it out on what amount you'll get or what insurance will pay, depending on who's at fault.

After you've called the insurance company, everything else sort of takes care of itself. You'll likely be told what shop to take your car to. If you need a car while yours is getting repaired, the insurance company will pay for it. Barring any injuries, your life will likely go back to normal soon enough.

WHAT SHOULD I DO IF I HIT A PARKED CAR?

You're driving in the parking lot and in a moment of carelessness you run into an unattended parked car. While it may be tempting to just hightail it out of there and let no one be the wiser, you should try to find the owner or at least leave a note for two very good reasons. First, it's just the right thing to do. You made a mistake that damaged someone's property, so you should shoulder the responsibility of getting the car repaired.

Second, you're required by law to find the owner or at least leave a note. Hitting an unattended parked car and leaving the scene without contacting the owner or leaving a note with your information constitutes a hit and run violation. If you were tracked down somehow (which gets easier and easier, especially with parking lot cameras and witnesses with smartphones), you'd likely face a heavy fine for leaving the scene of an accident on top of having to pay for the damages you caused when you hit the car.

So what's the protocol if you a hit an unattended parked car?

First, get out and assess the damage. If you totally smashed the car, you should probably go ahead and call the police. But if it's just a fender bender or busted taillight, there's no need to call the cops. With your cellphone camera, take lots of pictures of the front, sides, and rear of the car you hit. You don't want the owner trying to milk you and your insurance company for damages you didn't cause.

After you've taken pictures and if it's possible, find the owner and give him your information, including your name, phone number, insurance company, and policy number. If you can't find the owner, leave a note on the windshield of the car with the same information. The vehicle's owner may or may not call you. They'll likely just call your insurance company to file a claim. If they do call and are irate, just stay calm, tell the person to get in touch with your insurance company, and hang-up.

DAY 13

Know How to Network

WRITTEN BY ANTONIO CENTENO

Young men will often start to focus on networking only when they are looking for a job. Perhaps it's after graduation, or with the loss of a previous job.

This is the wrong way to think of networking – and the reason why so many people think of it in a negative light.

True networking is about giving. When you do so, a natural byproduct will be others giving back to you.

WHAT BUSINESS NETWORKING IS NOT:

- Putting in effort only when you need something, such as a job or a sale. You will come across as a taker. Nobody wants to be around a man who grabs everything for himself without contributing.
- Arriving at an event, handing out 50 business cards in 25 minutes, and then heading out the door hoping that you convert a few "prospects" into sales.
- Showing up to a job fair with 1,000 other applicants and jockeying for position so you can pitch a recruiter for 30 seconds on why you are the man for the job.

SO WHAT IS NETWORKING?

Business networking is the art of managing mutually beneficial relationships. It's about giving value, and receiving value in return. It's a long-term process. One that a man cultivates over an entire career and protects with his good name.

Professional networking, in its essence, boils down to two things:

1. Building Awareness
2. Being Referable

PART 1: AWARENESS – THE IMPORTANCE OF BEING VISIBLE

My family uses two vehicles, a truck (mine) and a minivan (my wife's). Every year I spend a sizeable amount of money on maintenance with a mechanic 30 miles away. There is also a great mechanic (from what I hear) who runs a shop one mile from my house. So why do I drive out of my way for this common service?

It boils down to awareness. In 2007, when I needed to make a decision about car repair, I only knew of the mechanic whose shop was across from my son's daycare, which just happened to be around 30 miles from my home in Shawano, Wisconsin. I walked in, was impressed with the owner's knowledge, and have been happy with his work ever since.

The point is, we generally hire the best people we can find within our network. We rarely hold out for the perfect job candidate, as businesses have to…well, do business.

So how do you get out in front of the person you need to be seen by?

AWARENESS TIP #1: ENGAGE YOUR CIRCLE OF INFLUENCE

Your personal network starts with the people you already know. For most of us that includes friends, families, co-workers past and present, and people we went to school with.

Stay in touch with all of them and let everyone know what you are looking for – whether it's a service need or a new career. You never know when someone is going to turn from a passing acquaintance into a useful contact. The internet has made keeping up with old acquaintances much easier; nowadays you have no excuse. Keep an eye on where all your old friends and classmates have moved to and what they're up to. Lightly engage with them and sincerely ask how their careers and lives are developing. Any deep relationship always starts with a shallow beginning.

Most people are passive about connecting with old friends or classmates, so you'll need to be the proactive one. Send real holiday and birthday cards and be sure to always send a nice note, or at least an email, for events like marriages, children, new jobs, etc. People really do remember these things.

You probably won't see much immediate reward for your diligence, but you'll be remembered more clearly than all the other old friends, relations, co-workers, and so on that haven't bothered to send the occasional greeting card or online message.

What this means is that you'll have the hard work already done when you need assistance from one of those friends. It'll also encourage them to come to you for favors, giving you a chance to increase your likeability as well as your presence in their life.

AWARENESS TIP #2: TALK TO STRANGERS

You never know where you're going to make a professional connection.

Increase your chances of doing so by being social when you're out in public. Talk to the person next to you at the hotel bar. Ask your local barista how they're doing. Circulate at parties and introduce yourself to new people, rather than clustering with the guests you already know.

The art of conversation is a forgotten skill, and it seems like most young men are content with putting their heads down and texting or checking their Twitter feed.

Break yourself of this habit.

Now I admit, talking to new people takes a bit of courage. Cultivate it. Practice approaching strangers, offering your hand, and simply saying, "Hi there! I don't think we've met. My name's ____."

This basic skill will work everywhere from a neighborhood tavern to a black tie gala. Be prepared to follow it up with simple, neutral questions like, "What brings you here?" Not everyone is good at talking to strangers, and you can expect to be the one guiding the conversation at first.

From time to time it won't come off right. You'll get someone who's shy, or snobby, or just distracted, and the conversation will end almost as soon as it begins. But the best thing about introducing yourself (and being good at doing so) is that you can move right on to the next person and do it again.

Master this skill in today's day and age and you'll be way ahead of most young men.

AWARENESS TIP #3: FOLLOW UP

Meeting people is great. But to actually network you have to get them to connect with you after that first meeting, otherwise you're just a fading memory (if that).

The best ways to follow up are:

1. Give out accurate contact information.

2. Give a reason for the other person to follow up with you.

For example: Business cards with basic contact info are a dime a dozen at conferences. But if you hand a person a card with a handwritten invitation, "Send me an e-mail and I'll see if I know anyone with an opening in your field," you're much more likely to actually get that e-mail.

Business cards are still the most convenient way to give someone your contact info (at least in person), but smartphones have made it possible to send an email, Facebook or LinkedIn invite, or other electronic contact right then and there. Make use of all the available options. Someone looking for a job (or to hire someone) is going to get more use out of your LinkedIn page, while a potential social contact will do better with your phone number and e-mail address. Also, be aware of your industry standards. If you're in San Francisco looking for a tech job, you'll want to be using the latest connection apps. If you're looking for construction management work in St. Louis, however, stick with business cards.

When someone gives you this sort of information, it's worth your while to do exactly what you'd want them to. Follow up on it the next day with a short email or phone call.

Some people are wary of giving out too much contact information publicly, which is a valid concern in this day and age. If you're worried about strangers having your information, it's worth getting a second phone line or email address that you can have printed on your business cards. That way you're never giving out the information you use with friends and families.

A small trick I employ is the use of a professional name (Antonio) with all my business associates and my nickname (Tony) with friends and family. This small separation allows me to quickly filter messages and phone calls.

Awareness Tip #4: Maintain Your Online Presence

Brett and Kate covered the subject of managing your online reputation very well in a previous chapter, but allow me to briefly touch on the topic again to discuss how it relates to networking.

To begin, let me be clear here – not all of us need to be using Facebook, LinkedIn, or any of the other social networks (and most of us could do well by not being on them every single day).

Some professions just don't need online networking, and some professionals selectively choose to remain offline in order to focus on business practices that worked for them well before the invention of the internet.

That said, the first thing many of us do before contacting a stranger is search their name online to see who they are and brush up on the relevant personal details, so it can pay to create a profile on social networking sites.

There are literally hundreds of social platforms out there. I'll talk about four.

> **LinkedIn** – This is by far the social networking platform most men should be on. It's not only a place to post your resume and work experience, but also a rich source of

news, business advice, and a great place to meet people before you attend networking events. Most of all, I want to stress that this is the right place for networkers because everyone on the platform understands that we're here to do business. It's not to socialize or read up on gossip, which can't be said for the others.

Facebook – If you have a personal profile, keep it private and never post anything you wouldn't want a prospective boss to see. If you're starting your own business or promoting a product, Facebook offers a huge upside, as it makes creating a business page simple.

Google+ – This newer network is much smaller than Facebook. I put it on this list because a profile on Google+ will give you a leg up in Google search results. If you're a young artist looking to show the world your portfolio, making it easily found on Google's preferred social network is a smart move.

Twitter – The network of instant information, these profiles pop up high in the search results but are best left for those looking to break into fields that actually use it. Public relations, marketing, and other media-type professions might take note if you show a mastery of this tool.

AWARENESS TIP #5: ACCEPT OFFLINE INVITATIONS

Get out there and physically meet people.

If a professional contact wants to have lunch and you can

spare the time, do it. If a friend has a poetry reading at the local coffee shop, go support her with an open mind. Stop by parties for at least a little while. And so on.

However strong your online networking skills are, the best contacts are still made face-to-face.

Large public gatherings expose you to people who you would never find a "shared interest" with using online profiles, but who just might have opportunities for you all the same.

Networking is unpredictable, and you never know who's going to turn out to be a stroke of blind luck.

PART 2: BE REFERABLE – THE IMPORTANCE OF OTHERS BEING ABLE TO PASS YOU ALONG

The power of networking isn't that you'll actually be able to pitch yourself to a prospective employer. No, the real power is that one of your connections will do it for you. Why?

Because referable men are valuable men. They have a definable skill set needed by certain groups, businesses, and individuals. An F-18 technician, a .NET programmer, a distance swimming coach — each of these professionals offers value and is referable. What they offer to the marketplace is clear.

Companies pay recruiters large sums to help find them the right people. If someone in your network refers you to the perfect job opening, they have delivered value to two people in their network – you, of course, but also the employer.

But how do you become someone who is referable?

REFERABILITY TIP #1: BE MEMORABLE

The most important tip to being referable is to be memorable. If a person doesn't remember what you do or how you can help others in their network, they can't refer you to their friends, even if they want to.

Have a tight 30-second elevator pitch about who you are and what you can offer. Also, if time permits, have an example success story to share. People remember stories, not facts and figures.

Example:

Stranger: "So Antonio, what do you do?"

Me: "Well you know how most men dress poorly?"

Stranger: "Yeah, sure."

Me: "Well I run a company that teaches men how to dress better so they can succeed in business. In fact, I just helped a young man last week from Iowa rebuild his wardrobe. He went through a round of five interviews over five days with a big consulting company in Chicago and never once had to worry about his clothing. He got the job. I like to think, in part, because he was able to focus in on what's important and not worry about looking like a kid from the cornfields."

At this point I've spoken for only 30 seconds. Yet, I've created a powerful and memorable image of who I am and what I do.

The man I'm speaking with doesn't need any clothing or help dressing sharp. However, 30 minutes later he introduces me to a colleague to whom he has already repeated my story.

The man I'm introduced to admits he needs to build a wardrobe – the perfect prospective client.

Be memorable, and when people find someone who needs your services they will make the introduction.

REFERABILITY TIP #2: DRESS TO IMPRESS

Your very first impression at any face-to-face meeting is visual. Everything else comes after that.

Being well-dressed makes you seem less threatening when you approach strangers, more influential when people are evaluating your usefulness as a contact, and more attractive to potential friends or romantic interests.

You certainly don't have to go through life in a business suit, and in fact you should be actively avoiding business wear when you attend social events (unless it's called for). But upgrading from jeans and a t-shirt to slacks and a dress shirt with a sports jacket for your default "around town" outfit can make a huge difference in your networking.

REFERABILITY TIP #3: OFFER SINCERE COMPLIMENTS

If you admire something about someone, there's no shame in telling them. It creates a feeling of goodwill, and people want to be around people who make them feel good.

The best compliments are based off a little research or close observation. Perhaps the gentleman you're speaking with is a newly hired teacher at a local junior college – congratulate him on the position and ask about the challenges he's facing as a new faculty member. Perhaps the woman to your left mentioned her book earlier in the night – point out that you admire the commitment writers have, and ask her to talk about the experience of being an author.

Never lay a compliment on too thick or expand beyond a simple one-sentence compliment. Use them to break the ice and then lead into a natural conversation.

At the end of the evening, what you talked about may be forgotten. The way you made others feel, though, is remembered.

REFERABILITY TIP #4: LISTEN AND SHOW INTEREST

Listen to what the people you meet are saying instead of just waiting for your turn to speak.

Ask intelligent questions and show a genuine interest in the conversation. This means that you stop checking your smartphone every three minutes to see if you received an email or text – it is a sign of disrespect. Personally, I turn my phone completely off at networking events to avoid temptation.

When you're first meeting someone you want to use the words "I" and "me" sparingly. You'll have to use them a few times, obviously ("My name is…"), but limit yourself. Resist the urge to identify with the other person's story by relating it to your life.

Instead, ask easy questions about the other person. If it's a business event, "What do you do?" is always reliable, as is, "How long have you lived in town?" It may take a few of these until you hit on the one that makes them expand beyond one-sentence answers, so always have a few of these questions ready to go in any conversation.

REFERABILITY TIP #5: BE OF SPECIFIC USE

The funny thing is that this last tip is the real reason why a person should hire or partner with you.

Why is it last on the list, then? In most networking situations you're not going to speak with the hiring manager right off.

Instead, you'll more likely find yourself in a conversation with one of their sales reps or other associates. If you start the conversation with a 15-minute one-sided discussion about how you can code in six programming languages, you're going to get the eyes-glossed-over look two minutes into the conversation.

Really, they don't care about the coding. And that's the problem. When networking, we try to ram our usefulness down other people's throats.

Rather than trying to impress, look to be of use. Ask about them and learn about their issues, then see if you can provide value from your wide range of skill sets.

Imagine if this same sales rep mentioned how a bug in their system continuously caused him and his team to show up unprepared to a client's office. Even though you haven't done this type of work for a year, you might be able to offer a solution they hadn't considered, and then 15 minutes later that same sales rep is introducing you to the hiring manager who was in another room.

Be a useful man and opportunity will seek you out.

IMMEDIATE ACTION – WHAT CAN YOU DO TODAY?

The best time to plant a tree is twenty years ago. The second best time is now.

I can't remember where I read this, but it is the best advice I can give a young man who is just starting and perhaps feels behind.

The simple answer is (and there is no way to shortcut this): you have to earn people's trust. That's how relationships have been, and will always be, built.

So start building your network today, right now. Ask for help, offer value, and maintain the relationships.

And remember, the best networkers build strong relationships before they ever need them.

Establish a Simple
Cleaning Routine
and Stick to It

During my first semester of college, I roomed with my good friend from high school in a dorm at the University of Oklahoma. We were pretty much like *The Odd Couple*, with me playing the part of the slobby Oscar Madison and my friend taking on the role of neat freak Felix Ungar, minus the annoying neuroticism.

You could walk into our dorm room and instantly tell whose side was whose. My roommate's side always looked presentable and clean: bed made, desk neat, clothes put away. My side looked like a disaster area: blankets and sheets askew, books and newspapers covering my bed, and laundry only half put away. The mess on my little twin bed sometimes got so big and unmanageable that I'd just sleep on top of all my crap, like you see those crazy people do on *Hoarders*.

Thankfully, my roommate was quite patient with me and kindly nudged me to start routines that would keep our place looking spic and span. I soon discovered that keeping things clean didn't take all that much time or effort. In less than 30 minutes a day, we created a haven of order and tidiness that would make Mr. Clean (and my mom) nod with approval. And my turning over a new leaf couldn't have come at a better time, as I started dating Kate soon after. It was nice being able to invite her over to our place without having to worry she'd be frightened to use a bathroom that looked like a giant petri dish of mold, bacteria, and other gunk.

For many young men heading out on their own for the first time, maintaining a cleaning routine on their own wasn't something they had to do at home. Sure, they might have helped with chores when asked, but they probably had their mom or dad telling them what to clean and when. Keeping your dwelling space clean and tidy is important for a variety of reasons: it's hygienic, allows you to feel comfortable having people over (and inviting in surprise guests), gives you peace of mind, and even helps conserve your supply of willpower.

Establishing a Simple Cleaning Routine

The key to keeping your place clean is to break the job up into smaller daily and weekly tasks. A lot of young men won't clean anything for a few weeks, and then when the mess gets so huge it can no longer be ignored, have to spend a whole Saturday digging themselves out from under it. Or, the job begins to seem so enormous they can't motivate themselves to tackle it, and let the mess grow even bigger.

Below, I offer a simple suggested routine for a young man living in a dorm or apartment that will keep your place clean while only requiring a small effort every day. It goes without saying that if you're living in an actual house, your routine will be a bit more complicated and involved.

What to Do Daily

Instead of letting messes pile-up, making them more of a pain in the arse to clean come Saturday morning, invest 10 minutes in the morning and 10 minutes at night in a daily cleaning routine.

Here's a suggested daily attack plan to keep your place in tip-top shape.

Morning

- Make bed
- Spray down shower with a product that keeps it cleaner for a longer period of time, like Method Daily Shower. Apply right after you get out.
- Wipe down bathroom sink and counter with a disposable Clorox wipe after you're done getting ready
- Empty dishwasher (if you have one)
- Wipe down kitchen counters and stove with a sponge and a 409-type product after you're done with breakfast

Evening

- Wipe down kitchen counters after dinner
- Spot vacuum
- Load dishwasher (or clean dishes by hand if you're in a dorm)
- Pre-bed clutter pick-up — go through the house and put away all the clutter you find before you turn in at night

WHAT TO DO WEEKLY

In addition to your morning/evening cleaning routine, do one bigger task each day of the week. Depending on the size of your place, each will take you 10-15 minutes.

Here's a suggested schedule:

- Monday: Dust
- Tuesday: Scrub toilets, shower, and bathroom sinks
- Wednesday: Vacuum and mop
- Thursday: Clean mirrors and windows
- Friday: Clean out leftovers and wipe down inside and

outside of fridge, wipe microwave inside and out, clean kitchen sink

- Saturday: Change and wash bed sheets

Adapt this schedule to fit your particular circumstances. For example, if you live in a dorm with communal bathrooms, you won't need to scrub the toilets and shower floors. But you can still dust and vacuum.

That's it. Together, the above routines only take about 30 minutes a day. If you have roommates, you can divvy up some of the tasks and shorten the time requirement even more.

Follow these routines, and your place will look great every day. All it takes is a bit of dedication and willpower to make these routines a habit, but the simplicity of this plan helps make it easier to stick with.

DAY 15

*How to Change
a Flat Tire*

Changing A Flat Tire: The Illustrated Guide

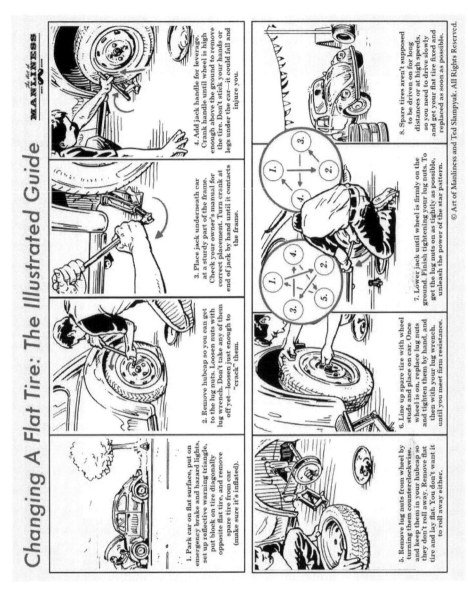

Maybe you have roadside assistance, maybe you don't. Either way, every young man should know how to change a flat tire himself. You never know if you, a loved one, or even a stranger, is going to need the help.

DAY 16

Create a
Budget

A lot of young men come to the realization that budgeting their income is harder and more complicated than they had imagined. After 18 years of having almost all expenses taken care of, figuring out how to live within your means on your own can be downright overwhelming.

I know I can remember a moment during my first month in an apartment by myself when I looked at all the bills I had due, and anxiously thought, "How in the heck am I going to pay for all this stuff?"

What I needed, and what all young men who are living on their own for the first time need, was a budget.

WHY CREATE A BUDGET

"Interest never sleeps nor sickens nor dies; it never goes to the hospital; it works on Sundays and holidays; it never takes a vacation; it never visits nor travels; it takes no pleasure; it is never laid off work nor discharged from employment; it never works on reduced hours ... Once in debt, interest is your companion every minute of the day and night; you cannot shun it or slip away from it; you cannot dismiss it; it yields neither to entreaties, demands, or orders; and whenever you get in its way or cross its course or fail to meet its demands, it crushes you."

–J. Rueben Clark Jr., "The Specter of Debt," 1938

When you're young and independent, your income is likely limited. You have to do all you can to stretch every last dollar. One tool that can assist you with that is a well-thought-out budget. A budget is basically a roadmap of your financial life. It allows you to plan your expenses so that you don't spend more money than you have coming in.

Without a budget, you may spend money on non-essential things early in the month and at the end of the month when bills come due, find that you don't have the scratch to cover them. At this point you're stuck, and may have to start charging things on your credit card to cover your outstanding expenses. Then, because you don't budget the next month either, you won't have the money to pay the balance on the card. Interest will start piling up, and you can soon easily find yourself in the enslaving grip of debt.

Creating a budget gives you control over the feeling of chaos you may have about your finances. Staying out of debt always involves difficult choices; you can't have it all. Creating a budget allows you to make informed, purposeful decisions as to how to allocate your money in the best possible way to reach your goals.

How to Create a Budget by Hand

Creating a budget by hand is pretty simple, but maintaining it can be difficult because of the discipline it requires. As I'll explain below, I personally recommend the online service Mint for creating and sticking with a budget. But I wanted to put the pen and paper option out there, because 1) some folks like doing things by hand, 2) going through the steps on how to create an offline budget is a good way of learning the basic principles, regardless of format, and 3) even if you don't plan on doing one by hand indefinitely, you might want to try it a few times in order to reinforce those principles.

1. Assess your monthly income. Gather your pay stubs together and figure out exactly how much you're bringing in each month. If you're self-employed or do work on the side, make a close estimate of how much you earn a month. You need to know how much money you have to work with before you start budgeting it out.

2. List your fixed expenses. Fixed expenses are those that stay roughly the same each month. They include things like rent, car insurance, car payments, health insurance, phone bill, and student loan payments.

3. Subtract your total fixed expenses from your total monthly income. The amount that's left over is what you can work with for your variable expenses. If your fixed expenses are more than your total monthly income, you're in trouble, as we haven't even gotten to your variable expenses yet. Cut the cable, downgrade your cell phone plan, get a roommate to reduce rent costs, etc.

4. Set a spending goal for variable expenses. Now that you know how much money you have to work with, you can start budgeting for your variable expenses. These are the expenses that fluctuate from month-to-month. Unlike fixed expenses, you have a degree of control over variable expenses; these are the areas where you can cut back the most and start getting ahead in your finances. This type of spending includes items like groceries, utilities, gasoline, eating out, and entertainment. Set a reasonable spending goal for each variable expense.

When you're just starting out in life, you'll likely be living paycheck to paycheck, and will understandably want to spend the remains of your variable budget on doing fun things with your friends after taking care of the basics like gas and food.

But as soon as you can swing it, make it a top priority to set aside a portion, no matter how small, to a retirement and an emergency fund. Let's face it, when it comes to retirement we can no longer depend on our jobs or the government to fund it; who knows what the future of entitlements will bring? Set aside a small amount each month when possible and put it into a Roth IRA or 401K.

In addition to saving for retirement, budget some money each month for an emergency fund. This money is to be used when you find yourself unemployed or to pay for car repairs and other unforeseen expenses; having one will give you a great sense of confidence and security. Even if you can only sock away $25 a month in the beginning, it's better than nothing. Most financial experts agree that you should save enough for three to six months of living expenses. That's hard to do when you're a young man, but again, just work on it slowly and do what you can. If you're looking for a good place to stash your emergency fund, check out CapitalOne 360 (formerly ING Direct). It's an online bank, and they have better interest rates than traditional brick and mortar institutions. It's what I use.

5. Subtract your total expenses (fixed and variable) from your monthly income. The goal is for your total expense amount to be less than your income. If it's not, you'll need to tweak your expenses so that they are. This may mean cutting back or cutting out things like going out to eat or cable television. If you have a surplus, put it into your emergency fund or towards your retirement.

6. Keep track of spending. After you've created the budget for the month, keep track of every single penny you spend to ensure that you stay within your budget. Keeping track of your spending will also come in handy when you make next month's budget. You'll be able to review how much you spent the previous month and adjust accordingly. This is probably the hardest part of budgeting, and where most people fail. I actually ditched doing my budget by hand a few years ago and switched to using Mint because I was terribly inconsistent with keeping track of my spending.

Track Variable Spending With the Envelope System

One of the best old-school methods of keeping track of your variable expenses is the Envelope System. It requires you to use cash for many of your expenses, which can be inconvenient at times, especially as more of our shopping moves online. But if it helps you to control your spending, then the inconvenience is worth it. Kate and I used the Envelope System when we were first married. Here's how it works:

Withdraw enough cash to cover your variable expenses like groceries and entertainment. Get some regular ol' mailing envelopes and label them "Groceries" or "Entertainment" or "Gas." Put the amount of money you've budgeted for each of those categories into its respective envelope. You can only use the money in the envelope when making purchases for that category. When the money runs out, you're done spending in that category for the month.

7. Review your budget every month. Each month, go over last month's budget to see how you did. You'll be able to see where you did well and where you can improve. After you review, repeat the whole process and make next month's budget.

My Recommendation: Automate Your Budget With Mint

As I mentioned above, I stopped budgeting by hand a few years ago and started using Mint.com to track my budget. In my opinion, it's the only way to go. Mint's free online service takes all the hassle out of one of the most important steps in budgeting:

tracking your spending. When you sign up for Mint, you'll be asked to connect all your financial accounts (checking, credit cards, loans, etc.) into their system. Don't worry. Mint uses the same 128-bit encryption and physical security that banks use. Their practices are monitored and verified by TRUSTe, VeriSign, and Hackersafe, and are supported by RSA Security. And besides, Mint is a "read only" platform. So if someone does hack into your account, they wouldn't be able to move money.

Track spending automatically. Once you have your financial accounts connected to Mint, just use your debit card as you normally would. Mint automatically tracks and categorizes your spending for you. So for example, if you pick up groceries at the supermarket, Mint will automatically categorize the purchase as "Groceries." It's almost magical how good Mint is at categorizing things automatically.

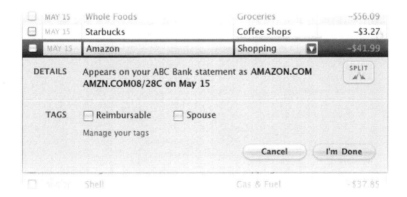

The system is flexible, so if you don't like the way it categorizes your spending, you can change it, and Mint will start organizing those transactions the way you prefer. There are times when the system gets things wrong or doesn't know how to categorize a transaction, but correcting it isn't difficult. Once the correction is made, Mint gets right back on track.

Tweak Mint's suggested budget. After a few weeks of tracking your income and spending, Mint will create charts and graphs that are easy to understand and show you exactly where your money is going. Using this information, Mint will create a suggested budget for you that you can then tweak to meet your financial goals. What's great about this tool is that as you adjust your budget, Mint will show you charts on how those changes will affect the amount of money you'll have left over at the end of the month, in real time.

Let Mint remind you if you're getting off track. Mint will send warnings to your email or cell phone when it notices that your current spending habits have put you on a trajectory that will overshoot your allocated budget. They'll also send you alerts when certain bills are due.

Review and adjust as needed. I log into Mint every week to see how things are going with my spending and budgeting. Mint's easy-to-read charts make reviewing a breeze. If I need to clamp down on my budget, I make the adjustment and Mint takes care of the rest.

THE 50/30/20 BUDGET RULE OF THUMB

As you sit down and put pen to paper (or finger to keyboard) to figure out your budget, you may find yourself getting overwhelmed by the minutia of it all or you may be left wondering if your budget is actually realistic. Sometimes it's helpful to have a benchmark or rule of thumb to compare your budget to see if you're on the right track.

One rule of thumb that I've found helpful when creating my

budget was coined by Harvard bankruptcy law professor (and now Senator) Elizabeth Warren. It's called the 50/30/20 Budget Plan and calls for the following:

- Limit 50% of your after-tax income to needs like rent, utilities, food, health insurance, and car insurance. You need to be really strict about what you classify as a need. A cell phone plan with unlimited data and texting isn't a need, cable isn't a need, and grass-fed buffalo steaks or SuperSonic burgers, while food, aren't needs either.
- Limit 30% percent of your after-tax income to wants. Clothes, eating out, cell phone plans, movies, subscriptions to magazines, apps, etc.
- Spend at least 20% of income on savings or paying down debt. If you have student loans or credit card debt, work on paying that down with at least 20% of your monthly income. Once you pay down your debt, shift to putting that money to retirement savings.

Again, this is just a rule of thumb to offer some guidance. You can adjust it if you want to be more aggressive with your debt repayment or savings. But if your spending roughly matches the 50/30/20 breakdown, you can be confident that you're on the right track financially.

BUDGETING FOR SOMETHING SPECIAL

In addition to the different kinds of fixed and variable expenses mentioned above, sometimes you want to budget for something special. Maybe you want to save up for a backpacking trip in Europe, a Saddleback briefcase, or an engagement ring for your girlfriend.

There is an awesome 1950s instructional film that reiterates some of the principles we've discussed, plus adds some other important principles of sticking to a budget — like fixing something to make it last longer, and buying quality instead of what's cheapest (we'll discuss this more in a later chapter). Watch it at this link: *http://youtu.be/FWQsBnzUvkQ*. It also offers a nifty idea on how to save for something special and keep track of how long it will take you to reach a goal: keeping a graph in a little pocket notebook.

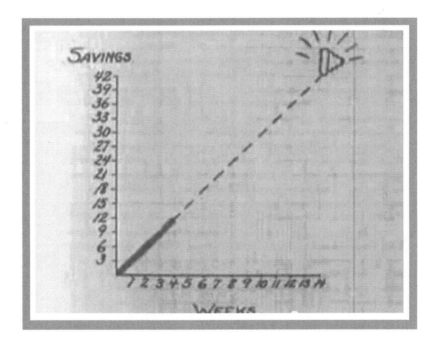

This is the kind of thing that's easy and fun to keep track of by hand. But Mint also allows you to track your savings for a special goal. First, you'll need to create a savings account that's just for your special savings goal. CapitalOne 360 allows you to easily create free sub-accounts for these types of goals. Once you create your special savings account, create a goal in Mint, and connect that goal to your special savings account. Mint will ask you how much money you want to save and when you need the money by. It will then spit out how much you need to save each month in order to reach it. As you save for your goal, Mint will let you know if you're on track to meeting it by your deadline. Pretty nifty indeed!

DAY 17

Essential Etiquette
for Young Men

—◆—

"In whatever society, or in whatever part of the world, a gentleman may happen to be, he always complies externally with the spirit and usages of the place... A gentleman always possesses a certain self-respect—not indeed touching upon self-esteem, and far removed from self-conceit...Indeed a gentleman, in the highest signification of the term, is a noble animal...Employing in the regulation of his own conduct, the strictest standard of propriety, and in his expectations of that of others, the most lenient; cautious in accepting quarrel, more cautious in giving cause for it; lending to virtue the forms of courtesy, and borrowing from her the substance of sincerity; forming his opinions boldly, expressing them gracefully; in action, brave, in conference, gentle; always anxious to please, and always willing to be pleased; expecting from none what he would not be inclined to yield to all; giving interest to small things, whenever small things cannot be avoided, and gaining elevation from great, whenever great can be attained; valuing his own esteem too highly to be guilty of dishonor, and the esteem of others too considerately to be guilty of incivility; never violating decency, and respecting even the prejudices of honesty;...full of courage, but free from ostentation; without assumption, without servility; too wise to despise trifles, but too noble ever to be degraded by them; dignified but not haughty, firm but not impracticable, learned but not pedantic; to his superiors respectful, to his equals courteous; kind to his inferiors, and wishing well to all."

– Richard Wells, *Manners, Culture and Dress
of the Best American Society*, 1894

Manners. Etiquette. For some men, these words don't belong in the same breath as manliness. For them, etiquette and manners conjure up arbitrary lists of dos and don'ts, a nagging mother, or scenes of artificial formality, complete with images of bowing and scraping, the polishing of monocles, and a bunch of treacly "How do you dos?" and "No, after yous!"

It wasn't always so. Our forbears saw no contradiction in being a rugged man and a refined gentleman. For centuries, well-bred men were trained in all the manly arts, from the skills needed to be a soldier to the proper etiquette for dinner parties. They were quintessential gentlemen—dapper in dress, polite in conduct, and yet every bit a true man.

George Washington, Theodore Roosevelt, and Robert E. Lee are some examples of men who combined gritty manliness with gentlemanly bearing. They paid attention to how they dressed, groomed, and conducted themselves and were as comfortable at a stately ball as they were on the battlefield. For these great men, having good manners did not make them less of a man, but more of one.

This is because they saw good manners in the way Edward John Hardy, author of *Manners Makyth Man*, defined them: as "little morals," "the shadows of virtues, if not virtues themselves." If character was the root of inner manliness, then manners were the outer fruits that sprouted from the tree — the external behaviors and code of conduct that naturally followed from a life of virtue. These great men understood that while it is true that the rules of etiquette change over time and from culture to culture, the underlying principles of all manners remain constant: a respect for others, and a desire to treat all people with honesty and consideration — just as you'd like to be treated.

Still unconvinced? First, let's take a more specific look at some misconceptions about manners, and then at the reasons you should cultivate them.

WHAT GOOD MANNERS ARE NOT

A young man's negative opinion on manners sometimes springs from observing others practice them badly. But these are not true manners, for:

Good manners are not stiff, formal, or awkward. Good manners should come off as entirely natural. Some young men, knowing this and not wanting to seem like they're trying too hard, swing the opposite way, and try so hard to be "natural" in their manners that they come off as even more contrived! Real naturalness comes from a few things:

- *Forgetting yourself and concentrating on others.* The more you focus on making others comfortable, the less self-conscious you will feel, and the more comfortable you will become yourself.
- *Catering your behavior to the crowd and event in which you find yourself.* Your manners should be more formal when visiting the White House than when eating at Chili's.
- *Practice.* Good manners shouldn't be something you cram for in emergencies like studying for an exam. Rather, they should be a habit you develop through practice over time, like a leather coat that gets softer, more comfortable, and

better-looking the more you wear it.

• *Cultivating an inner sense of character.* This is most important. At its root, naturalness in manner springs from your sincerity and desire to treat people well for the right reasons; as mentioned above, it should be a natural extension of your character. Even if you do end up being a little awkward, if it comes from a sincere place, people will be very forgiving of it.

Good manners are not ostentatious. Good manners should never be showy or call attention to themselves. In fact they should not even be immediately noticeable in the moment and instead should create an overall positive impression, which the people with whom you interact only reflect on later: "I really enjoy his company." "I had such a good time at his party."

Good manners are not smug and judgmental. You don't practice good manners to feel superior to others or to wield them as a club, policing people's behavior. As Charles Dickens once wrote: "My boy," said a father to his son, "treat everyone with politeness—even those who are rude to you. For remember that you show courtesy to others not because they are gentlemen, but because you are one."

WHY PRACTICE GOOD MANNERS?

Good manners give you confidence. Much of what constitutes good manners consists of common sense. Yet common sense can often fail us when we're nervous, in unfamiliar territory, or just winging it. Look at manners as the signposts along the broad highway of common sense, guiding you in how to act and react in any situation without veering off and getting lost in the thickets when you're not sure what to do.

Good manners make a positive impression on others. A man with good manners makes enjoyable company, a welcome party guest, a referable contact, a trusted employee. Good manners attest to a man's self-respect and self-control, qualities that apply to all areas of life. Plus, as good manners are in such short supply these days, they instantly put you head and shoulders above other young men out there.

Good manners add *texture* to life. In our day-to-day lives, we often just move from one thing to another, as each day bleeds into the next. Thus from time immemorial people have sought a break from the ordinary by creating festivals, rituals, special occasions. But special occasions aren't special if we behave and dress exactly as we do in our everyday lives. Manners provide a unique texture to our lives, and contribute to adding a special atmosphere to special events – the solemnity of a funeral, the pomp of a wedding, the grace of a baptism, the significance of a graduation, even the escape of a movie. At the same time, creating this atmosphere is a community effort – with the guy in a t-shirt and shorts, the ringing of a cell phone, or the man walking in late, the spell is broken.

Good manners make things in life smoother, more pleasant, and more comfortable for everyone. Ironically, manners both add texture to life, and make our interactions smoother. Many old etiquette books describe manners as the substance that "oils the creaking wheels of life." While we'd like to think that left to our own devices, everything would just flow naturally between people, without these guidelines on how to act – who does what and when – a whole lot of awkwardness and impoliteness ensues.

Good manners make other people feel comfortable. Ever been at a dinner where a guy brought up embarrassing stories from someone's past, or insisted on pontificating about politics? Have you ever been with a friend who started talking to someone who was a stranger to you, but never stopped to introduce you to him, leaving you standing there awkwardly? "For what is a good manner?" William John Hardy wrote, "It is the art of putting our associates at their ease. Whoever makes the fewest persons uncomfortable is the best mannered man in the room."

Good manners ultimately show respect for others. Do you like to wake up early to meet someone, only to have them be 20 minutes late? Do you enjoy it when your friend throws a tantrum after losing a round of golf? Would you like it if you made $2.50 an hour, busted your butt serving people, and then got stiffed on a tip? Do you appreciate being interrupted while you're speaking? No? Then live the heart of good manners: the Golden Rule. Treat others with the same respect you'd like to be treated with.

In summary, good manners make life richer and more enjoyable for you and for others. Unfortunately, many young men are raised with very little guidance on the proper manners to cultivate for different areas of their lives. The good news is that good manners can be learned by any young man no matter his background (and by any older man, no matter his age).

We've written about the basics of etiquette extensively in the past, and while we still have a few areas to hit, have covered nearly all the essentials. So we put together an etiquette study guide for a young man seeking to become a more dignified gentleman. Visit this URL for all the links to the subjects mentioned below: *www.artofmanliness.com/category/a-mans-life/etiquette*.

ESSENTIAL ETIQUETTE FOR YOUNG MEN

ETIQUETTE OF SPOKEN COMMUNICATION
How to Debate Politics Civilly
The Dos and Don'ts of Conversation
How to Avoid Conversational Narcissism
How to Listen Effectively

ETIQUETTE OF WRITTEN COMMUNICATION
How to Write a Letter
How to Write a Sympathy Note
How to Write a Thank You Note
How to Write an Email That Will Get a Response
Being a Gentleman in the Age of the Internet: 6 Ways to Bring Civility Online

ETIQUETTE IN THE ARENA: ON THE FIELD AND AT
WORK

How to Celebrate with Grace

How to Lose with Dignity

A Guide to Sportsmanship

The Dos and Don'ts of Business Etiquette

ETIQUETTE FOR EVENTS

A Man's Primer on Funeral Etiquette

A Gentleman Never Arrives Empty-Handed

A Man's Guide to Dining Etiquette and Proper Table Manners

Dinner Date Etiquette

How to Be a Gracious Host

How to Be the Perfect Houseguest

How to Be a Perfect Party Guest

How to Be the Perfect Party Host

SOCIAL ETIQUETTE

How to Shake Hands Like a Man

How to Make Introductions

The Importance of Being on Time

The Reasons You're Late and How to Always Be on Time

How and When to Open Doors for a Woman

How to Apologize

10 Ways to Be a Gentleman at the Gym

Guide to Tipping

The Unclassified Laws of Etiquette

STYLE ETIQUETTE

Dressing for Life's Big Events: How a Man Should Dress for Weddings, First Dates, Religious Ceremonies and More

Dressing for the Occasion: 60 Second Visual Guide

How to Dress for Different Meetings

What to Wear on a First Date

What to Wear on a First Date: 60 Second Visual Guide

DAY 18

Renting Your
First Apartment

—◆—

One of the first "adult" things you'll likely do when you head out on your own is rent an apartment. The process can be a bit intimidating for first-timers. Below we take you through the steps of finding an apartment, navigating the legalese of the lease agreement, as well as managing your rights as a tenant.

FINDING AN APARTMENT

Figure out how much you can afford. Take a look at your monthly income. Experts recommend only spending between 25%-35% of your after-tax income on rent and housing. So let's say your pay, after taxes, is $1,500 a month. Ideally, you shouldn't pay more than $525 a month on rent.

You also need to take into account that you may be responsible for some of the utility costs of your rental. So you'll need to figure in another $100+ to cover those costs.

Keep in mind that some apartments have income requirements that will put you out of the running altogether.

If you can't find a place within your budget, consider getting a roommate.

Create criteria for your ideal apartment. What are you looking for in an apartment? Do you want a studio or a single bedroom? Maybe you want to rent a small house? Do you need the apartment to come with appliances, including washer and dryer? Do want it to be close to school or your work? Do want it to be within walking distance of retail, like groceries or coffee shops? Are you willing to live in a neighborhood known for its crime levels?

Write down whatever comes to your mind. While you might not be able to get everything on your apartment wish list, it will definitely help in narrowing down the possibilities.

Identify potential apartments. With your list of criteria in hand, hop online and start searching for apartments. When Kate and I looked for an apartment here in Tulsa, I simply began the search by Googling "Tulsa apartments for rent." Google actually brings up a map that pinpoints apartments or homes for rent in your city. That map makes narrowing down potentials pretty easy because you can see if the apartments are close to work or school, near grocery stores, or in safe areas of town.

Once you narrow down apartments by location, check to see if they have the things you're looking for in a rental, i.e. appliances, number of bedrooms, etc. Most big apartment complexes have a web page where you can look at floor plans, the amenities they offer, and the cost of rent. Smaller units might only have a phone number. Give them a call and ask about their available units and cost.

Don't just limit your search to Google. Make sure to hop on Craigslist to find homes or apartments that might be for rent by individual owners as opposed to bigger companies.

A couple of other good sources for finding potential apartments are rental magazines that you can pick up for free at supermarkets, as well as *rent.com*. If you find your apartment using the latter, they'll send you a $100 gift card. Bonus!

Set aside a day to visit your potentials. You'll want to visit your potential rental units in person to see their condition and possibly submit a rental application. Make this process as efficient as possible by visiting as many of your potentials as you can in a single day. Saturdays are the busiest days for landlords showing apartments, so try to go sometime during the week. It's best to call the landlords and set up an appointment with them, but if you can't, most buildings will give you a tour anyway. You'll want to set aside about 45 minutes for each visit, so plan your appointments accordingly.

VISITING PROSPECTIVE RENTALS

Make a good first impression. When you visit a potential apartment, the landlord or apartment manager will be evaluating you as much as you're evaluating them. They want to make sure the people they rent to are reliable, courteous, and easy to get along with. Your first impression starts with the phone call to set up the appointment. Be polite and speak clearly.

When you actually go visit the apartment, dress for the occasion. While you don't have to wear a shirt and tie, you shouldn't come rolling in to your appointment wearing sweatpants and a crummy t-shirt. Nice jeans and a polo will work well.

Be on time! If you show up late to your appointment, the manager or landlord could take that as a sign you may be late in paying rent.

When you meet the manager or landlord, offer a firm handshake, a warm smile, and thank them for meeting with you.

As you look at the rental unit, keep your comments positive and your possible complaints close to your vest. No need to spout off a list of upgrades and requests before you're even offered the place. That will just scare landlords away from you. Wait to bring up your concerns until after you've been accepted as a renter.

Check for problems. As you walk through the apartment, check the following things, but again, don't broadcast your concerns right away:
- Look for signs of mold, mildew, and insect infestation.
- Open and close all the doors and windows, and also check that the locks function properly.
- Flush the toilet and run the water in the sinks and showers. Pay attention to water pressure and temperature.
- Look for obvious damage like broken fixtures, holes in walls, broken tile, etc.
- Check for wear and tear in the carpet.

Ask questions. While you should keep small concerns to yourself about the unit while looking at it, feel free to ask the landlord or apartment manager any questions you might have that will help in your decision-making process. Here are some possible questions you may consider asking:
- What's the monthly rent?
- Are any utilities included with the rent?
- How much is the security deposit?
- When is rent due? Do you have auto-pay?
- What's the make-up of the other tenants? Are they mainly younger students? Married couples with families? Older folks?
- Have you had any break-ins in the past year? Are car break-ins a problem?

- What's the parking situation like? Do you pay for a parking spot?
- Do you take care of small maintenance issues or am I responsible for some of the repairs in the apartment?
- Am I able to re-paint the walls or make other modifications?

Again, be friendly and polite when you ask these questions. No need to be combative.

Ask current tenants about their experience. Online apartment reviews are pretty worthless in my experience. It seems the only people who leave reviews are folks who had a bad experience with the landlord or apartment manager. And when you read the reviews, you often get the sense that this person is a little unhinged and probably had a hand in creating the problem they're griping about in the first place.

To get a better idea of what it's like to rent at a particular complex, it's best to ask current tenants. When you're visiting, and don't have a person from the office by your side, ask any tenants you may run into about their experience living there. Is the landlord easy to work with? Are they responsive to repair requests? Do they feel safe living here? Are the neighbors quiet and friendly?

FILLING OUT THE RENTAL APPLICATION

When you find a place you like, you'll likely have to fill out a rental application. Landlords and apartment managers use the application to screen potential renters. The application will ask about your employment and monthly income as well as your rental history. You'll also be asked to sign a consent form giving permission to the landlord to run a background and credit check. Be completely truthful when filling out the application! Any fibs on it will likely be discovered during the background check, resulting in your application ending up in the trashcan.

And to be clear: submitting a rental application in no way obligates you to anything. If the manager approves it, you'll then be asked to come in to the apartment office to sign a lease.

Check your credit history before submitting a rental application. Landlords are allowed by law to check the credit histories of potential renters to screen for people who are or aren't likely to pay rent on time. If they see that you've had trouble paying bills on time, that's a red flag that they shouldn't rent to you. It's good to check your credit history before submitting an application so you can correct any mistakes that may adversely affect you in the rental process.

Be ready to pay a rental application fee. Landlords are allowed to charge you an application fee to cover the cost of the credit check. The fee should be in the $20-$30 range; anything more, and you're probably getting ripped off. If you're submitting multiple rental applications, the credit check fees can quickly start adding up. To curtail those costs, you might consider getting your credit report yourself and making copies of it to give to landlords. Some may insist on requesting the report themselves, out of worry that you may have doctored the copy to make it look better than it actually is. But you may be able to persuade a few to accept your copy, thus saving you some money. It doesn't hurt to try.

Have a list of references ready. You may be asked to provide a list of personal and professional references. Have those ready and make sure to tell your references they should expect a call from a landlord.

Signing the Lease (or Rental Agreement)

After your rental application has been approved, the landlord will ask you to come to the office and sign a lease. This is where you can bring up any concerns you had about the rental unit, as well as negotiate for better terms or perks. You need to be on your game during this time, because once you sign your name on that dotted line, you're pretty much stuck with the terms written in the lease.

Have enough money in your checking account to cover the security deposit and first month's rent. When you sign your lease, the landlord will usually ask that you pay a security deposit as well as the first month's rent. Make sure you have enough money available (they may only take cash, money order, or debit card) to cover both amounts. The security deposit will be stored in a savings account during the term of your lease. If you terminate the lease early or leave the apartment in disrepair, the landlord will use the security deposit to cover those costs. If you leave the apartment in the same condition as you got it, you can get your security deposit back. More on that later.

Difference between a lease and a rental agreement. Leases and rental agreements are pretty much the same thing except for one thing: time. Rental agreements typically go from month-to-month, while leases last for a longer period of time, usually a year. Landlords are free to raise the rent at the end of each month when a rental agreement expires; leases lock in the rate of rent for an entire year.

If you know that you'll only be in the apartment for a short period of time, ask for a rental agreement; if you plan on staying in your place for at least a year, get a lease.

Read the lease or rental agreement before signing! Don't sign anything until you've read through the lease line-by-line. You want to know exactly what you're getting into when you agree to rent from a landlord. Make note of anything you find disagreeable, and ask questions about what you don't understand. As you read through it, look for the provisions that answer the following questions:

- How much is rent? Duh.
- How much is the security deposit and how can you get it back? Understand what sort of condition you'll need to leave the apartment in if you want to get your security deposit back.
- What's the term of the tenancy? Month-to-month? Nine months? One year?
- What happens at the end of the lease? When the term of the

lease is up, what do you have to do to renew it? How much will the landlord increase your rent by? If the lease is up, but you still need a place to stay for a month or two, can you ask that the lease convert to a month-to-month rental agreement?

• What happens if you terminate your lease early? This an important provision to check. Sure, you may plan to stay in your apartment for a year, but plans can change and you'll have to terminate your lease early. Most apartments will ask for 30 to 60 days notice if you plan on terminating the lease early. Pay attention to see if there are any termination fees. Under the law in most states, you are legally responsible to pay the landlord only for the actual loss in rent that your early termination caused. So if you move out early, and it took the landlord a month to find another renter, you'd be responsible for one month's rent.

• Many corporately managed complexes will try to sneak in clauses saying you have to pay two or three months rent for ending a lease early. Because they can often fill the vacancy quickly, they end up scoring a huge windfall — they have two months rent from you, plus rent from the new guy. That's illegal in most states. If you see termination fees like that in the lease, try to get them deleted or modified before you sign. Forfeiting your security deposit and paying a month's rent is usually a reasonable termination fee.

• If you have signed with a roommate, are you jointly and severally liable? Usually when you sign a lease with a roommate, the lease will state that each co-signer is jointly and severally liable. This means if your roommate doesn't pay his share of the rent or moves out before the end of the lease, you are still on the hook for the full amount of the rent.

• Where, how, and when is rent paid and what happens if you're late on rent? You'd be surprised, but some landlords are really particular about how rent is paid. They want it in a certain form (check, credit card, etc.) and deposited in a certain place. Make sure you know where and how this is to take place. Also make sure the lease is clear on when rent is due and what happens if you pay late. Most landlords will charge a fee on late payments.

• Which utilities are you responsible for? Some landlords cover the cost of all utilities, while others cover none. Many will have arrangements where they'll pay the water bill, but then tack on your portion of the bill to your monthly rent.

• Is subletting allowed? Let's say you take a three-month trip during the summer. You have a friend who needs a place to stay during that same three-month period. Instead of leaving your apartment vacant for three months, you offer to let your friend stay in your place as long as he pays you the amount of monthly rent so that you can pay the landlord. You just sublet. Most landlords prohibit subletting, but some allow it. If you think you'll need to be able to sublet to someone else, make sure the lease allows you to.

• Are you allowed to make alterations to the dwelling? You're not the owner of the property, so you can't replace counters or paint the walls without the landlord's permission. Most places I've rented from allow you to paint the walls, as long as you paint them back to the original color before you move out.

• Are you responsible for minor repairs or is your

landlord? While landlords are required by law to make repairs that ensure the dwelling is habitable, they're not required to take care of minor repairs, and may leave that to you to take care of. Most large apartment complexes will fix just about anything in your unit. In leases with individual landlords you'll often see clauses stating that the renter is responsible for minor repairs.

- Are pets allowed, and if so, do you have to pay an extra fee for having one? Some apartments allow pets (often with size restrictions); some don't. The ones that do often charge an extra monthly fee.
- Is smoking allowed? Landlords are allowed to prohibit smoking in their units. If you're a smoker, you'll want to know that before you sign the lease.

Get any oral promises in writing. If the landlord made any oral promises to you while you were looking at the apartment, get those promises written in the lease. You never know when your complex will be under new management, in which case they would not have record of a verbal agreement of a special provision made just for you.

Feel free to negotiate and delete any of these terms. If you see any terms you don't like, ask to have them modified. Also, feel free to negotiate the rent amount or security deposit. Before you and the landlord sign the lease, anything is fair game to change in the contract.

Inspect the Apartment Before Taking Possession

Before you take possession of the apartment, the landlord should give you a Landlord-Tenant Checklist that lists all the rooms, fixtures, and appliances in the apartment. Inspect the apartment and make note of the condition of the various items on the list. If you notice any damage, make sure to photograph it, and point it out to the landlord or manager. Be as thorough as possible during this inspection. This will protect you from forfeiting your security deposit for damage that already existed before you took possession.

Get Renter's Insurance

Renter's insurance covers any loss to your personal property due to robbery or accidents. It also covers any damage you might cause to other tenant's property. For example, let's say your washing machine springs a leak and water seeps through the floor and ruins your neighbor's antique dresser. Renter's insurance would cover that.

When you sign your lease, your landlord may strongly suggest and even hint that you're legally required to get renter's insurance. Their concern isn't for your benefit. The landlord wants your insurance policy to pay for any damage or injury that your negligence causes instead of the aggrieved party suing the landlord. While you're not required to have renter's insurance in most states (except Virginia), it's a good idea to get it anyway. As Woodrow Call from *Lonesome Dove* would say: "Better to have it and not need it, then to need it and not have it." Renter's insurance will set you back about $15-$25 a month, less if you tack it onto another policy (like auto) you have with an insurance company.

Your Rights and Responsibilities as a Renter

Court cases and state statutes have established rights and responsibilities that you have as a renter. If your landlord violates any of these rights, you're entitled to recourse.

Renter's Rights

You have the right to a habitable premise. While you're not entitled to five-star amenities, you do have the right to rent a place that's habitable. What constitutes a habitable premise? Case law and statutes generally define it as having the following attributes:

- safe structural elements including floors, walls, roofs, and secure doors and windows
- all electrical, plumbing, heating, and air conditioning systems function
- working hot and cold water
- exterminating infestations of rodents and other insects
- access to trash receptacles

If your apartment ever suffers any defects that make your place inhabitable (like sewage backing up in your bathtub), your landlord has a duty to fix it. While some apartments let you make online requests for repairs, as well as provide a phone number for "emergencies," always make sure you document your request in some way. The landlord will then have a certain amount of time to make those repairs. If they don't, you have several recourses, such as withholding rent until the repairs are made or paying someone to fix the problem and then deducting the cost of repair from your rent. It's when you decide to go those routes that having your communications with your landlord well documented becomes so important.

You have the right to privacy. While the landlord owns the property, they can't barge in anytime they want. All states have laws stating renters have a right to privacy while renting. Pretty much the only time the landlord can come into your rental without permission or notice is when they're responding to an emergency that threatens injury or property damage.

Any other time the landlord wants to enter your apartment, they need to have your permission and in some cases, give you 24-hours notice before entering. Some landlords or apartment managers will try to bully you into giving permission. Don't give in. If your landlord bugs more than is reasonably necessary and fails to comply with requests to leave you alone, you can sue your landlord for invasion of privacy or breach of "implied covenant of quiet enjoyment."

You have the right to a safe premise. The landlord can't prevent all crimes or accidents that occur on their premises, but if the crime or injury occurred because of the landlord's negligence, you can sue them for any damages or costs you may have incurred.

Renter Responsibilities

In addition to the provisions in the lease agreement, many states have statutes on the books listing the responsibilities of the renter.

Keep the premise clean, safe, and in good repair. This is the most common responsibility you'll see listed in statutes. Basically, you're required by law to take care of the apartment while you're a tenant there. Not too hard.

Reimburse the landlord for any damages you may cause. If you don't keep the apartment clean, safe, and in good repair, you have the responsibility of reimbursing the landlord to make the apartment clean, safe, and in good repair again.

Getting Your Safety Deposit Back When You Move Out

So your lease is up and you're ready to move on to greener pastures. How do you get that $500 security deposit back? In my experience, most landlords will try to do anything to ensure that they don't pay back your deposit.

First, clean your apartment as well as you can, including carpet cleaning if possible (landlords will often clip you on this). Second, get your Tenant-Landlord Checklist that you filled out when you first moved in and run an inspection again with your landlord. You can't be charged for ordinary wear and tear that comes with living in an apartment, but you can be for damage and excessive filth.

If they try to charge you to replace something when a repair would be sufficient, object. Also, if you paid a cleaning a fee before moving in, your landlord can't deduct your security deposit for any cleaning.

If the landlord does have to deduct from your security deposit to replace and clean your apartment, you're entitled to an itemized statement that explains the purpose of each deduction. If you think any of the amounts are excessive and unwarranted, push back and make your case. If your landlord won't change his mind, unfortunately your only recourse is to take him to small claims court. Make sure you have everything well documented, though, should you choose to do this.

The landlord has 14 to 30 days after you move out to return your security deposit.

DAY 19

Fix a Running Toilet

WRITTEN BY DARREN BUSH

Fsssssshhhhh...

"Just jiggle the handle..."

Have you heard that before? Yep, that wonderful sound of a rogue toilet. You lift the lid, poke things a little, and hope the pot fixes itself.

My late father had many fine qualities, but aside from knowing which end of the hammer was for hitting, he was not a handyman. If something broke, he would rig it as best he could, but since this was before duct tape, his solutions were sometimes more creative than effective. Replacing toilet guts might as well have been brain surgery.

Even if you're not "handy," you can fix a running toilet rather easily, and many other things as well. The key is the right tools, the right parts, the ability to read, the discipline to not take short cuts, and patience.

The truth is that a toilet is a simple thing. There are two moving parts: the float and valve assembly, and the stopper that controls the release of water. When you release 1.6 gallons of water, it splits between the top of the bowl and the bottom, creating a Venturi effect that sucks down (hopefully) the waste.

But moving parts wear out, bend, come loose, or just give up the ghost. If your toilet is running or not working, take the following steps.

1. **Check the connection between the handle and the stopper valve.** A chain of some sort will connect the handle with the stopper, and pushing the handle opens

the stopper valve. That's why jiggling the handle will sometimes help the stopper close properly, but it's not a permanent fix. If the chain is disconnected entirely, the toilet will obviously not flush.

2. Check the stopper valve. It should easily flop into its "seat" and seal the tank. If the stopper valve is not seating properly, then the toilet runs and wastes a lot of water. Sometimes you can tweak the hinge on the valve to get it to seat properly. If not, it'll need replacing.

3. Check the float. The traditional float is a big ball at the end of a rod that controls the valve that fills the tank after a flush. More common these days is a donut-shaped float that slides up and down on the overflow tube, or an internal float that shuts the water valve when it hits a certain level. Either way, if the tank isn't filling up as much as needed to flush properly, make sure the float isn't leaking. If it is, it'll need replacing.

Let's say all your poking and prodding isn't doing the trick. Lucky you! You get to replace the toilet guts. So go buy the toilet guts. You can get them almost anywhere. No need to be a plumber, just go to the local hardware store and ask for toilet guts (or something like that). They are almost always sold as one unit, and they're inexpensive enough that you can replace the whole thing easier than replacing specific parts. You may also decide to replace the supply hose, since you're already messing around there.

You can spend a lot or a little. The expensive ones are quieter, but other than that, it doesn't matter. Fifteen bucks will do the job. It's a toilet.

REMOVE OLD TOILET GUTS

1. Pee. The sound of all that water flowing will no doubt cause an increase in urgency.

2. Disconnect the flushing handle from the stopper on the inside. It should be a simple chain or other mechanism you can do by hand.

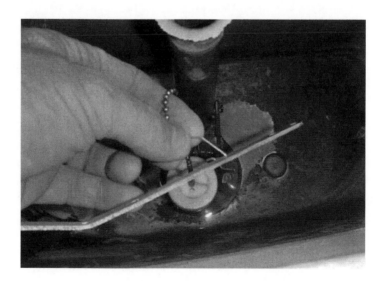

Note the crusties around the top of the drain tube. Just some calcium, not part of the pipe. It'll break right off. If you're highly OCD you can nuke the whole tank with vinegar. That said…*it's a toilet.*

3. Shut off the water. The valve below the toilet gets very little use. Sometimes it's a little corroded or encrusted with hard water minerals, since the last time it was used was when the toilet was installed or the mechanism replaced. A little vinegar and a soft wire brush can clean it up a little. Close it tightly. Place an old towel or bowl under the faucet to catch water when you unhook the supply hose.

4. Drain the tank. Flush the toilet by reaching in and pulling the stopper up. The tank will not refill because you shut the water off. To keep things a little neater, you could sponge out the remaining water and wring it into the bowl. It makes for less dripping later. You'll notice I use braided, steel-covered supply lines. They're probably overkill, but it's cheap insurance. Your mileage may vary.

5. Loosen the supply hose at the valve. Use a proper wrench…not a crescent wrench. Let it drain into a small pan. Then loosen the supply hose at the fitting under the tank. This is usually a plastic nut or wing nut that you can hand-tighten or loosen. If it's really stuck, carefully use a pair of Channel Locks to urge it along. Proceed carefully here.

6. Loosen the big, plastic nut under the tank where the supply hose entered. It's a bigger plastic knob that attaches the guts on the inside of the toilet. Water will leak out here, but it's clean water, just like from the tap. Continue to loosen it and remove the guts.

7. Pull off the old stopper thing. Congrats, your toilet is now dry and useless. Time to fix that problem. Here's the dead one below.

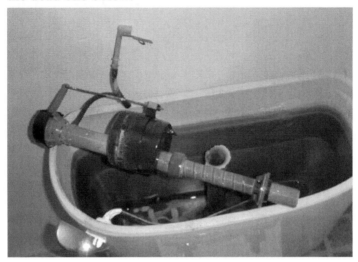

Install New Toilet Guts

1. Reinstall the new guts by dropping it through the hole in the tank. There should be quite a bit of gasketing here. Make sure the area is clean so the new gasket seals properly. Get a friend to hold it in place while you tighten the big nut underneath the tank. If you overtighten it, you might crack the plastic, so just go until it's snug.

Proper building code says that the overflow tube has to be at least an inch above the full level. Different assemblies adjust differently. The one picture below adjusts by twisting the whole mechanism and sliding it up and down, then twisting to lock it. The float is internal in that white part that sticks off to the side of the water feed.

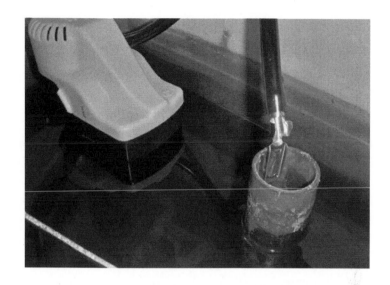

2. Attach the supply hose to the bottom of the tank. Finger tighten only, but do turn it until it stops. No need to use Teflon tape here; it's plastic to plastic. No wrenches.

3. Attach the supply hose to the faucet. Here it's metal to metal, so use a bit of Teflon tape. Just wrap the threads, then re-attach. Non-crescent wrenches work best.

4. Turn the water on, check for leaks. Your fill hose should squirt into the overflow as noted. The tank won't fill here, you're just checking your connections. Turn the water off.

5. Install your new stopper by pushing the plastic studs on the overflow tube through the soft rubber of the flapper. It should go on easy.

6. Reattach the chain from the stopper to the toilet handle, adjusting the chain so it is as taut as possible without lifting the stopper. Test by flushing a few times. The stopper should drop on its seat when the water reaches the bottom of the tank. If it doesn't, adjust it a little until it does so consistently. When it doesn't seat, that's when you have to jiggle the handle to get it to do so. That's what we're trying to avoid.

7. Clean up. There will be black goo on things. That's not what you think it is — it's just deposits that form inside the tank over time.

That's it. Your toilet is now operational again, simple as that. Drink a few beverages of your choice and test it again. Congratulate yourself on a job well done.

DAY 20

*Maintaining
Your Car*

If you had access to a car while living at home, chances are your parents took care of its maintenance or offered reminders as to when to take it in for service. When you're on your own, car maintenance becomes your responsibility. Yes, it can be expensive and time consuming, but the investment you make today will save you money down the road.

Don't be like the 1/3 of college students who change their oil less than two times a year because they simply forget to do it. Your car won't magically take care of itself. Get in the habit of regular car maintenance and quit relying on your folks to remind you to get your tires rotated or your oil changed.

Below we take you through some of the rudimentary things you should be doing to ensure your car stays in tip-top shape.

EVERY OTHER FILL-UP, DO THESE THREE THINGS

Instead of standing at the gas pump and reading the advertisements for a credit card while you wait for your tank to fill, use that time to give your car a quick check-up (and cleaning) by performing three simple tasks:

1. Clean windshield. A dirty, bug-splattered windshield is a safety hazard, as it obscures your view of the road. So give it a regular cleaning. Using the spongy part of the gas station squeegee and soak the whole windshield with the cleaning fluid. Then pull the squeegee tightly from the middle of the windshield to the sides, finishing off the remaining streaks by pulling it top to bottom. This is especially important after an extended drive on the highway when your windshield is littered with insect carcasses and using your car's washing fluid and wipers to remove them only creates a big, smeary mess that obscures your line of sight even more.

If your headlights are dirty, give them a squeegeeing as well.

2. Check tire pressure. Maintaining proper tire pressure will keep you safe and even save you a little dough. Improperly inflated tires — and this may mean over-inflated or under-inflated — don't handle or stop as well as tires with the correct pressure. They also increase your chance of a blow out. Plus, tires with the correct pressure have a longer life and increase your fuel efficiency.

You'll often find your vehicle's recommended tire pressure on a sticker inside the driver's side door. Car manufacturers spend a lot of time coming up with this number, and it's the one you should use.

Tire pressure is something you have to keep your eye on, as it constantly changes as the tires log miles and the temperature fluctuates. That's why it's so important to check it regularly and add air when needed. Some experts say you should do this at every gas fill-up, but just as with the oil check, every other fill-up should be enough to catch any deficiencies before they become big problems.

Checking your tire pressure takes less than two minutes. Here's how to do it:

- **For an accurate reading, always check tire pressure when your tires are "cold,"** that is, before you've driven around on them. I only check my tires' pressure at a gas station when I fill up at the one less than a mile from my house, first thing in the morning. If you've already been driving around for awhile, let the tires "rest" for at least four hours before checking the pressure.
- **Find out the tire pressure recommended for your car (it's in your owner's manual and on a panel inside the driver's side door, as pictured on the previous page).** Always fill the tires to this recommended level, regardless of tire brand, and not to the max PSI found on the tire sidewall – that number indicates the maximum pressure the tire needs to carry its heaviest load, not the tire's ideal PSI.
- **Check tire pressure with tire pressure gauge**
- **Fill when needed**

3. Check oil level and top off as needed. Motor oil is essential to your car's performance. Its most important job is to lubricate all the moving parts in your engine so they don't grind and tear themselves into dysfunction. It also transfers heat away from the combustion cycle and traps and holds all the nasty byproducts of combustion, sending it to the oil filter. If your engine doesn't have enough oil, your car is at risk of going kaput.

To ensure your car always has enough oil, it's important to get in the habit of regularly checking it. Your owner's manual probably recommends that you do this at every gas fill-up, but every other is typically sufficient. Checking your car's oil level is super easy. All you need is a clean paper towel, adequate light, and about three minutes. You should save this job for last because you need to wait about five minutes after you turn the engine off for the oil to drain back into the pan:

Before checking your oil level, make sure your car is on level ground so you get an accurate reading. Locate your engine's dipstick. It usually has an image of an oil can or just says "OIL."

• Pull the dipstick out. No snickering.

• Wipe it clean with a paper towel. The gas station usually has some available near the pumps.

• Back goes the dip stick. Make sure it goes all the way in.

• Now, we're actually going to check the oil level. Pull the dipstick out again, but don't turn it upside down to look at it. This makes the oil run upward and ruins your reading. The dipstick will have two marks at the bottom. They are usually either lines or holes in the stick. Mine has two holes. The oil level can be read by looking where the oily part ends and the dry part begins. If the oil line is between the two marks, you're good to go. If it's below the bottom mark, you need to add some more oil. Just a quart, mind you. You should never add more than a quart at a time without driving and taking a new reading of the oil level. Too much oil isn't good for the engine. There you go. You just read a dipstick.

Most cars are designed to consume a bit of oil between changes, and many manufacturers consider a consumption rate of one quart every 1,000 miles to be normal. Some cars lose more than that because of leaks or because the engine is burning oil along with the gasoline. If you're needing to add a quart of oil every 500 miles or so, you should take your car in ASAP to get it checked for external and internal leaks.

FOLLOW THE MAINTENANCE SCHEDULE SUGGESTED IN YOUR VEHICLE'S OWNER'S MANUAL

Your vehicle also requires maintenance tasks that are performed less frequently, but are vital to allowing your automobile to live a long and fruitful life. These tasks include oil changes, tire rotations, replacing transmission fluid, and the like.

Don't follow a dealer's or mechanic's recommended maintenance schedule. They often suggest that you come in more frequently and perform maintenance that you really don't need. For example, most quick lube and dealership service shops recommend you bring your car in every 3,000 miles for an oil change, despite the fact that most modern engines are designed to run for 5,000 miles before needing one. Another example is coolant replacement. A lot of mechanics recommend having it replaced every 30,000 miles, but many vehicles don't need this service until they reach four times that. And after the 120k mark, manufacturers often recommend the coolant be replaced only every 60,000 miles.

Instead of relying on Larry at the KwikLube to tell you when you should service your car, pop open your glove compartment (or "jockey box" for you gents living in the Mountain West region), and pull out your owner's manual. There should be a section where it lists the manufacturer's recommended maintenance schedule, which tells you how often to get your oil changed, rotate the tires, and replace fluids and parts. If you can't find the owner's manual, a quick Google search will bring it up. By following your vehicle's ideal maintenance schedule, you can prevent costly inspections, repairs, and replacements, and keep your car humming for many years.

DIY Car Maintenance

As newer vehicles have become increasingly complex with onboard computers and high-tech gadgetry, maintenance jobs now often require a mechanic with the proper training and tools to correctly complete the task.

But there are still a few maintenance jobs that most men can do themselves on most models, and below I list three of the most accessible. It's true that taking care of these tasks doesn't save you very much in either time or money, but it is satisfying nonetheless and I recommend trying each job at least once, as they'll give you a reason to look under your hood as well as a small bit of insight into how your trusted chariot works.

Change oil every 5,000 miles. We've written a guide on how to change your car's motor oil yourself. But for those living in an apartment or dorm, this might not be an option. Whether you do it yourself or take it to a mechanic, getting your oil changed regularly is one of the most important ways of keeping your car running smoothly.

Change air filter every 12,000 miles. This is quite possibly one of the easiest car maintenance jobs you can do yourself. Regularly changing your car's air filter will increase fuel efficiency, prolong your engine's life, and reduce emissions.

While changing your car's oil comes with the hassle of finding a way to dispose of the used oil properly, no such inconvenience exists for the air filter, and doing it yourself will easily save you half the cost of having a service shop take care of it.

Rotate tires every 5,000 to 10,000 miles. Front and rear tires wear differently. Regularly rotating your tires equalizes their natural wear patterns, ensuring a smoother and safer ride. It also extends the life of your tires, which will save you money on costly replacements.

To learn how to perform all of these yourself, visit: *www.artofmanliness.com/category/manly-skills/cars*

KEEP YOUR CAR CLEAN

Besides performing regular maintenance, another important part of taking care of your car is keeping it clean.

Wash your car regularly. Every day our cars are subjected to sun, salt, grease and grime, acid rain, smog, tree sap, dead bugs, and worst of all, the acidic compound of bird poop bombs. These things eat away at paint, and once that's gone, they will eat at the metal in your car. While failing to wash your car won't result in immediate damage, over time the elements will corrode your vehicle, along with its potential re-sell value.

How often should you wash your car? It depends. Location and climate are the two biggest factors in determining frequency. If you live in an area with a lot of pollution and sea salt in the air, you'll need to wash it two or three times a month. If you live inland and in an area with little pollution, once a month will suffice. During the winter, you may need to wash your car more frequently than you do during the summer due to the snow, salt, and mud that will accumulate as you drive along icy roadways.

Don't forget to detail your car after you wash it!

Don't use the inside of your car as a garbage can. The inside of your car is not a garbage can, so quit treating it like one. Get in the habit of regularly cleaning out your car so it doesn't constantly look like a dump. Keeping your car's interior clean and tidy can reduce stress in your life and make the driving experience more enjoyable. Also, you never know when you'll have unexpected passengers. By keeping your car clean, you'll never have to sheepishly say, "Sorry about the mess," as you wipe away shards of yesterday's QuickTrip breakfast burrito from the passenger seat.

DAY 21

Know Your Way
Around a Kitchen

—◆—

If there remains a lingering sense among older generations of men that cooking is "women's work," I would think it is probably fading greatly among the younger set. True, for much of human history men did the hunting/farming and women did the cooking, and this arrangement continued to work well into the 20th century. Young men made a quick transition from living with their flapjack-flipping mother, to settling down with a meatloaf-making wife. Or, he lodged at boarding houses that provided victuals along with a bed.

But those days are long gone; accommodations that come with a cook are now virtually non-existent (although it lives on in fraternity houses), and men are remaining bachelors longer – well into their late 20s and early 30s. As all modern men still need to eat virtually every single day, the only choice that remains is either starving…or being completely *dependent* on restaurant meals and take-out food.

Maturing into a grown man means becoming self-sufficient, so daily dependence isn't an option. Further, not only does learning to cook help you become more independent, it offers other benefits as well:

Keeps you healthy and strong. When you cook for yourself, you know and control exactly what you put in your mouth. Almost anything you make for yourself, even the same dish served at a restaurant, will have less salt, fat, calories, and additives than the commercially-made variety.

Saves you money. Sure, it is possible to eat cheaply by ordering all your food off the dollar menu, but while fast food won't clip your wallet, it will take a toll on your health, which will cost you big bucks down the line. When it comes to making real, wholesome food, cooking at home is generally cheaper than eating out.

Impresses the ladies. As a young man, you're going to be dating, and nothing impresses a gal like a man who can invite her back to his place for a home-cooked meal.

Gives you enjoyment. No, I don't always enjoy cooking. But when you have time and are in the right mood, it can be very satisfying to create something tasty for you and your friends/family.

Now, I'm not a cooking zealot. Sometimes the way I feel about cooking can be summed up in a comic from The Oatmeal (*theoatmeal.com/comics/cook_home*); it can seem like it is more hassle than it's worth, and when you're super busy and stressed, the convenience of take-out is a lifesaver. The key is striking a balance, and you can't do that if you can't cook anything beyond toast and ramen.

The good news here is that while gourmet chef-ery takes a lot of training and practice, simple cooking can be learned by anyone who knows how to read. So in this chapter, we cover many of the basics a young man who's never cooked for himself needs to know to get started. First we'll talk about how to stock your kitchen with equipment and your pantry with staple items. Then we'll talk about a few basic skills and bits of know-how you need to learn in order to cook edible, hopefully delicious, food. Finally, because you don't need to amass the kitchen equipment listed below all at once, we'll talk about some things you can cook when your options and tools are limited.

Let's get started.

STOCKING YOUR KITCHEN: ESSENTIAL EQUIPMENT

For this section, I had AoM's food writer, Matt Moore, give us the lowdown on how to outfit your kitchen. Here's what he had to say:

> For me, it's always about quality over quantity. Instead of investing in specialty garlic presses, zesters, or other gimmicks – just give me a killer knife that'll do all those jobs and not get lost in my junk drawer. Less is always more.
>
> For that reason I've put together my list of essential kitchen equipment needed for every guy. You don't need to go out immediately and stock your kitchen with everything listed here. You can acquire this stuff over time. Be resourceful and check yard sales, flea markets, or online outlets that offer these items at great deals. Meanwhile, improvise and make the most of what you have.

1. **(1) Small 2.5-qt Pot with Lid** - terrific for making sauces, steaming veggies, or heating liquids.

2. **1 Large 6-qt Pot with Lid** - perfect for boiling pasta or potatoes.

3. **9×13 Pyrex Baking Dish** - a must-have for baking or roasting.

4. **12-Inch Cast Iron Skillet** - cast iron cookware is inexpensive and will last a lifetime. On top of that, it cooks evenly, retains heat, and is also believed to keep you healthy by supplying a steady dose of iron to your diet.

5. **12-Inch Non-Stick Skillet with Glass Lid** - the non-stick surface makes cleanup quick and easy.

6. **Dutch Oven-Style Pot with Lid** - enameled cast iron is the best option; however any pot with a heavy bottom will do the trick. Great for making soups and braising meats.

7. **Grill Pan** - a fantastic substitute for a grill. I prefer cast iron grill pans over the non-stick versions.

8. **Non-Stick Baking Sheet** - super cheap, and probably one of my most utilized items in the kitchen.

1. **8-Inch Chef's Knife with a Sharpening Steel** - a chef's best friend. Don't go cheap here.

2. **Can Opener** - I prefer the manual ones – still never figured out the electronic versions.

3. **Box Cheese Grater** - I like these because it provides several different options in one; a slicer, a rough grate, a fine grate, and an extra fine grate for harder cheeses. Choose one with a large base to provide more stability.

4. **Food Processor/Blender** - the workhorse of the kitchen. Great for saving time and creating specialized dishes.

5. **Pepper Mill** - indispensable for any kitchen. Fresh cracked pepper is worth the extra effort, and this tool makes it easy to always have it on hand.

6. **Measuring Cups and Spoons** - these will be absolutely necessary to make sure you are getting the right measurements when following recipes.

7. **Pot Holder/Oven Mitt** - because I don't know anyone who likes to burn themselves. A folded towel will also work.

8. **Spatula** - my preference is stainless steel slotted spatulas.

9. **Tongs** - great for when you need a more precise touch.

10. **Vegetable Peeler** – fantastic for peeling fresh vegetables or shaving cheeses.

11. **Wine Opener** - I prefer the ones that also have a bottle opener. A drill, drywall screw, and pliers will do the trick if you find yourself in a bind. Trust me.

12. **Potato Ricer/Masher** - a ricer is a great tool for making silky smooth mashed potatoes. A masher is an

even cheaper and more versatile tool that will provide a more rustic consistency.

13. **Digital Meat Thermometer** - a useful tool to make sure your meat is always perfectly cooked.

14. **Cutting Board** - I prefer a large wood cutting board over any other surface. Make sure it has a solid footing, so as not to slide while cutting.

15. **Whisks** - extremely versatile; fantastic for making vinaigrettes, dressings, or even a roux.

16. **Wooden Spoon** – heatproof and durable, I like having these in several different sizes.

17. **Colander** - a must-have for draining, washing, straining, or rinsing.

SERVING/STORAGE ITEMS: FOR THE CUPBOARDS

1. Flatware
2. Assorted Serving Plates or Platters
3. Assorted Mixing/Serving Bowls
4. Storage Containers
5. Storage Bags
6. Plastic Wrap
7. Aluminum Foil
8. Wax/Parchment Paper

Thanks, Matt! Now let's take a look at stocking your pantry.

STOCKING YOUR PANTRY: THE ESSENTIALS

HEADING OUT ON YOUR OWN

These are the things that will come in handy for a variety of recipes or a spontaneous meal idea, and are always good to have on hand.

1. All-purpose flour
2. Baking powder
3. Baking soda
4. Brown sugar
5. Honey
6. Oats
7. Sauces (soy sauce, BBQ sauce, hot sauce, etc.)
8. Cornstarch
9. Peanut butter
10. White sugar
11. Olive oil
12. Cans of beans
13. Diced tomatoes/tomato paste/tomato sauce
14. Herbs and spices (salt, pepper, Italian & Mexican seasonings, crushed red pepper, garlic powder, onion powder, curry powder, chili powder, basil, cilantro…whatever seasonings you enjoy)
15. Instant broth (cans or cubes)
16. Pasta and other noodles
17. Rice

HOW TO READ A RECIPE

It's true (and is often said) that all you need to know in order to cook is how to read a recipe. But how do you read a recipe? These tips will up your chances of culinary success.

1. First things first, read through the recipe in its entirety. It's easy to look only at a recipe's ingredients before deciding to make something. But when it comes time to prepare the dish, you may find you don't have a tool or ingredient that may only be mentioned in the directions, or that it's a lot more complicated than you thought, and a little above your pay grade. If the recipe includes terms you don't recognize, look them up.

2. Add up how much time it will take. Be sure to check out the "prep time" (slicing, stirring, can-opening) and "cook time" (baking, frying, grilling). Add them up to find the total time needed to complete the dish. If it's your first time making a certain recipe, it will definitely take you longer than the given time; give yourself an ample cushion.

3. Make sure you have all the ingredients. If you think you might have something already, but aren't sure, check to see. Also make sure it's still fresh. Then write a list of all the ingredients you don't have on hand.

4. Take note of what you need to do *before* the preparations begin. Before you start slicing, dicing, and mixing, you may need to do things like preheat the oven, soften butter, or defrost meat.

5. Set out all of your ingredients and tools. Line up everything you will need: bowls, pans, and utensils on the counter, ingredients measured and ready to go. This will not only make things smoother as you go along, saving you from dashing to and from the fridge and the cupboards, but it's basically a chance to check-off the recipe's ingredient and supply list one more time; you don't want to get halfway through your preparations, only to realize you're 1/4-cup short of the required 1 cup of flour.

MEASURING INGREDIENTS

DRY MEASUREMENTS VERSUS WET MEASUREMENTS

When a recipe calls for a 1/2-cup of this, and 2 cups of that, the tool you reach for depends on whether the ingredient is dry or wet (if it's pourable – oil, sauce, milk — it's wet).

There are two options: wet measuring cups and dry measuring cups. While they technically each hold the same volume, there are reasons why you should choose one or the other for respective ingredients.

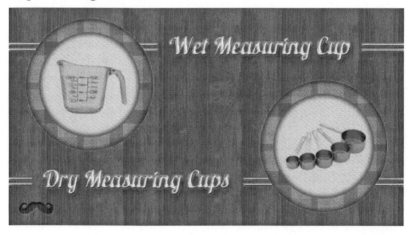

A liquid measuring cup has small measurement gradients printed up the side, and the top fill line sits well below the spout, so you don't spill any liquid when you pick up the cup. When you fill a wet measuring cup, don't hold it in your hand – put it on a level surface and squat down to make sure the liquid is sitting right at the desired mark.

Dry measuring cups are meant to be filled up to the very top, and then leveled off with a knife. If you filled a dry measuring cup to the very brim with a liquid, you'd be bound to spill some. And if you used a wet measuring cup for a dry ingredient, you wouldn't be able to level it off.

Here's how you fill a dry measuring cup with a few common ingredients:

- Flour — lightly spoon into cup and level off with knife. Don't tap the cup to settle, or pack in with spoon or fingers.
- White sugar — scoop directly from bag/container. Level off with knife.
- Brown sugar – scoop and then press with back of a spoon until the sugar is level with the brim of the cup.
- Peanut butter/shortening – pack with spatula (spraying the cup with cooking spray before using PB will result in it sliding out easier).

TABLESPOONS VERSUS TEASPOONS

A common mistake beginner cooks make is to confuse the tablespoon with the teaspoon, as they are often abbreviated in recipes in different ways, and these abbreviations are very similar. You may see any of the following:

- Tablespoon: T, tb, tbs, tbsp, tblsp, tblspn. (May be capitalized or lower case.)
- Teaspoon: t, ts, tsp, tspn. (Almost always lower case.)

A tablespoon is larger than a teaspoon. In the US, one tablespoon equals three teaspoons.

You can use tablespoons and teaspoons for both wet and dry ingredients. A recipe may call for a level or rounded amount; rounded roughly sits above the rim of the spoon, level is done by scraping off the top with a knife.

BUTTER

A stick of butter will have the measurements printed on the wrapper of each stick. Just mark off what you need and cut through the butter, wrapper and all.

BASIC COOKING SKILLS EVERY YOUNG MAN SHOULD MASTER

There are tons of cooking techniques out there, and down the road you may want to learn to make a soufflé or smoke some ribs. But it really only takes a few basic how-tos to keep yourself well-fed and happy.

KNIFE SKILLS

Diced, minced, chopped…what's the difference? The handy photo below illustrates these different terms using a red pepper as an example.

How to Make Pasta

Pasta is an especially good option for young men; it's cheap, versatile, and relatively good for you (depending on what you add to it). It's also really simple to make. At least, it should be. But I didn't realize I was making it wrong until after I got married; Kate was aghast to see me put the pasta in right after filling up the pot with water, instead of waiting for the water to boil; a recipe for mushy pasta. Here's how to do it right:

> **1. Use about 5 quarts of water for a pound of pasta.** That sounds like a lot, but a common mistake is to use too little water, which leads to the pasta sticking and clumping together. When planning your mealtime, keep in mind that that much water takes a while to boil, especially because you want to start with cold water (as it absorbs the least amount of impurities from your pipes).

2. Choose a pot that will leave you some room on top, so the water doesn't boil over. 5 quarts of water in an 8-quart pot works well. If all you've got is a 6-quart, just keep a close eye on it.

3. Bring water to a rolling boil. This means it's boiling across the whole surface of the water and you can't stop the boil by stirring it. Putting a cover on the pot will help it reach this point faster.

4. Once boiling, add two tablespoons of salt. The salt boosts the boiling temperature slightly and adds a little flavor to the pasta. But fear not — it only raises the pasta's sodium content a tiny bit.

5. Add the pasta, and stir it around immediately to keep it from sticking together, as the strands release their starch as they hit the heat. Stir the pot again every few minutes until pasta is done.

6. Consult the pasta package for relatively accurate cooking time. A minute before the minimum given cooking time on the package is up, fish out a strand with tongs and bite into it. The consistency you're looking for is "al dente" (Italian for "to the tooth") – tender, but with a little bite. Keep in mind that the pasta will continue to cook a bit even after you remove it from the heat.

7. As soon as the pasta reaches desired doneness, dump it into a colander. Pick up the colander and give it a few shakes to get the water out. But don't overstrain it – a little wetness works well with sauce. Don't rinse the pasta either (unless you're making a cold pasta salad), as it rinses away the starch that coats each strand, and this starch will help the sauce stick to the pasta.

8. Toss pasta with sauce immediately, if you can. If you can't, toss the pasta with a little olive oil to keep the strands from sticking to each other.

How to Make Eggs

In my opinion, eggs are one of your best resources in the morning. Full of quality protein, virtually carb-free, and packed with vitamins and minerals, they make the ultimate breakfast food. Don't be too swayed by the cholesterol scares of the 1980s; eating the whole egg–not just the whites–has actually been shown to have anti-inflammatory properties and to improve good cholesterol levels. Eggs are a fantastic food for men who are looking to get in shape; they help build your muscles, and they keep you satiated for a long time. A study showed that men who ate eggs instead of carb-rich bagels for breakfast consumed less calories over the course of the day.

And besides their great nutritional profile, eggs are easy to prepare, taste great, and are dirt cheap (less than 15 cents per egg!).

Scrambled. Whisk eggs in a bowl with either a fork or a whisk; mixture is ready when evenly colored. Heat skillet over medium-high and add butter or oil. When pan sizzles, add eggs. Wait until eggs have set a little bit and use wooden spoon or rubber spatula to "scramble." Done when there is no longer any runniness.

Fried. Heat a skillet over medium-high. Add oil to skillet. Crack eggs into pan, allowing each egg to cook separately. After a minute or two, the transparency of the egg will be firm and white. At this point, cook until desired yolk firmness achieved. Poke yolk with your finger to determine doneness.

Omelet. Chop desired veggies, meats, etc. and cook over medium-high heat in a skillet for 3-4 minutes. Whisk eggs like you would for scrambled, and add to skillet. This time, instead of scrambling, keep egg portion all as one. Tilt pan back and forth so runny parts spread evenly. When eggs are mostly set, flip with spatula. Add cheese to one half, cook additional 45-60 seconds, then slide out of pan onto plate, folding the omelet in the process.

How to Make Bacon

Ahhhh bacon, that most wonderful of man foods. There is just something about bacon that men love. Perhaps it is the sizzle of the bacon in the pan, or that hunger-pang inducing aroma that fills the house when the bacon hits the heat. Whatever it is, one thing is for certain: most men love bacon.

Classic Pan-Fry. Let bacon sit out of fridge for several minutes. Place in skillet over medium heat. Flip once, about ten minutes in. Continue cooking until desired crispiness attained. Remove and lay on paper towels to absorb excess grease.

Microwave. Lay your strips of bacon on three paper towels on a microwave-safe plate. Cover arrangement with one additional paper towel. As a general rule, cook one minute per slice. If your microwave does not have a rotating tray, rotate the plate at least once while cooking.

Professional. Preheat over to 350 degrees F. Lay bacon on cooking sheet without overlapping. Bake 10-15 minutes, but keep an eye on it for desired doneness.

Vermont Style. Place several slices of uncooked bacon into a bowl and douse with maple syrup. Place in fridge for 30 minutes to "marinate." Then, pan fry. Beware, this style is slightly more messy.

Brown Sugar "Cure." Let bacon warm to room temperature. Coat both sides in brown sugar and let sit for a few minutes. Use classic pan fry and enjoy the delicious results.

How to Make a Burger

The key to burgers is quality ingredients. Fresh 80/20 ground chuck is a safe bet.

- With your hands, loosely form as many 6oz patties as you're cooking.
- Use your thumb to create a dimple in the middle of the patty;

this ensures the burger cooks evenly without plumping.

- Season with salt and pepper, and other seasonings of your choice.
- Grill burgers over high heat; avoid using a spatula to press down, this ensures the flavorful juices stay in the burger.
- Flip just once, grilling 3-5 minutes per side depending on your desired doneness.
- When done, allow burger to sit for a couple minutes so the juices re-distribute through the burger.

WHAT CAN I MAKE WITH...?

Even if heading out on your own means setting up camp in a college dorm with a meal plan in hand, that doesn't mean cooking can't have any place in your life for the next two semesters. There will be times when you don't feel like making your way over to the cafeteria or food court, and times when they won't be open, leaving you to pillage the dorm vending machine. And unless you have an unlimited meal plan, making some meals for yourself can save you money.

Of course whether you're headed to a dorm room or perhaps a tiny studio apartment that only offers a kitchenette, or you do have access to a kitchen but not the assortment of appliances and pots mentioned above, you may feel like it isn't possible for you to make anything with such limited room and equipment. But with a little creativity, you can truly whip up some tasty stuff for yourself with only the most spartan of supplies.

Below we offer a few suggestions for things you can make if you only have one or more of the following appliances.

What Can I Make with a Fridge and a Hot Pot?

This is the situation many college freshmen will find themselves in; dorm rules often allow students two appliances in their rooms: a small refrigerator and a hot pot (an electric kettle that quickly boils water). Obviously the number of things you can make with these appliances, beyond ramen and mac n' cheese, is limited, but there are still options:

Salad. Get some salad makings; raw veggies, pre-cooked chicken, and dressing – toss together.

Cold sandwiches. You don't have to limit yourself to bologna and cheese, either. There are hundreds of really good sandwich combos out there. Don't forget wrap sandwiches too – get a Caesar salad kit, mix, add some precooked chicken, mix, and wrap.

Oatmeal. Get the kind that's not quite old fashioned whole oats, but are a step up from instant. Add nuts and dried fruit.

Hard boiled eggs. Portable and nutritious snack.

Canned soups. Easy, nutritious, and can hit the spot on a winter's day.

What Can I Make with a Microwave?

Some dorms allow microwaves in students' rooms, or have a common microwave for all to use. It is a surprisingly versatile tool — good for more than heating up your Hungry-Man dinners.

Scrambled eggs. This was a staple of mine freshman year, and not as bad as you might think. Scramble the eggs in a bowl, and nuke for 60-90 seconds, stopping to stir once or twice. Add salt, pepper, and ketchup to taste. You can also poach and "fry," eggs this way. But never cook them in their shell, as they can explode, and always prick the yolk if you leave it intact.

Bacon. What are eggs without bacon? Layer a plate with three paper towels, place bacon strips on top, and cover with another paper towel. Cook at about one minute per slice.

Bean and cheese burrito. Warm up some refried or black beans and layer in a tortilla with cheese, guacamole, salsa, sour cream...whatever your heart desires.

Rice+Tasty Bite/Soup. You can make instant rice in the micro-wave, or they even sell pre-cooked rice in a package that only needs to be warmed up. Add some beef stew or Tasty Bite Indian food on top of the rice. The latter is a good option for vegetarians.

Pizza bagels. Better in a toaster oven, for sure, but fine in a pinch.

Corn on the cob. Yes, you can actually make it in the micro-wave. Wrap each cob in saran wrap, and microwave for 2-3 minutes per ear. It's that easy.

Steamer meals. You add meat, veggies, and sauce to a spe-cial Ziploc steam bag, and steam in the microwave. Sample recipe: Beef fajita strips, pineapple, onion, bell peppers (red, green, yellow), BBQ sauce.

WHAT CAN I MAKE WITH A GEORGE FOREMAN GRILL?

Obviously George's Lean Mean Grilling Machine is adept at cooking things like burgers and chicken breasts, but it handles meats like bacon and sausage patties as well, along with making good grilled cheese sandwiches, paninis of any variety, and tasty quesadillas too. I wouldn't go out of my way to get one though – it's one of those things that sounds handy, but will end up gathering dust on a shelf. At least it did for me.

WHAT CAN I MAKE WITH A RICE COOKER?

A rice cooker is basically a steamer and a hot plate, and if you have a microwave and a hot plate (or regular stovetop), you don't need one, unless you enjoy using it and have the space. But you might live in a dorm that allows rice cookers, but not hot plates, and if that's the case, take heart; despite the name, this appliance can cook a lot more than the white stuff – eggs, spaghetti, chicken soup, and even taco meat and spare ribs can be whipped up in one. They're all just a Google search away.

WHAT CAN I MAKE WITH A CROCKPOT?

The ladies have been all over crockpotting lately, and it's perplexing more men don't adopt this cooking tool, as it's one of the easiest, least time-intensive methods of cooking available. One of my favorite crockpot meals is stupidly simple: plop in a couple of chicken breasts, pour some BBQ sauce over them, and then let it cook on low for six hours (or on high for four).

When it's done, you shred the chicken, and pile it on some Texas Toast. Delicious. I also enjoy making easy beef stew: throw in some stew meat, cut-up potatoes, carrots, and green beans, and then some V8 juice and other spices to taste. Press cook. Go about your day. Enjoy your stew hours later.

Hundreds of other tasty crockpot recipes are only a Google search away.

WHAT CAN I MAKE WITH A HOT PLATE/STOVETOP AND ONE POT?

If you have a hot plate or stovetop, but your cookware is limited, do a search for "one-pot meals." These are just what the name implies, and they make clean-up a snap. Easy chili is one of my go-tos: brown hamburger meat at the bottom of the pan, add a can of drained pinto beans, diced tomatoes, and a packet of chili seasoning. Simmer for 10-15 minutes. Done. I like to ladle mine over some Fritos and top with cheese. It's not going to win any prizes in a chili-cooking competition, but it's really satisfying on a cold winter's day.

BUT, BRETT! I DON'T EVEN HAVE ANY OF THE THINGS ABOVE! IS THERE ANYTHING I CAN MAKE FOR MYSELF?

Maybe you're living in a dorm that's super strict about appliances in rooms. Well, there is one trick you can use…get out your iron. Yes, the one you use to get the wrinkles out of your shirts.

Iron-Made Grill Cheese

First, I'll show you how to make a classic comfort food staple, the grilled cheese, using an iron in your dorm room.

What you need: an iron, a towel, aluminum foil, butter, two slices of bread, and two slices of cheese.

- Heat up the iron to its highest setting (no steam!) as you get things together. You'll want to use a towel or some other protective surface.
- Butter the bread.
- Tear off a piece of foil that is big enough to wrap your sandwich. Put down the first slice of bread — butter side down! — on the foil.
- Slap on two slices of cheese, and then put down the second slice of bread — butter side up! — on top.
- Wrap up the sandwich in the foil. You don't want your grilled cheese getting on your iron.
- Place your iron on top and let it sit there for 1-2 minutes. Cook time will depend on how hot your iron gets, so the first time you try this, check on it 45 seconds in to see how it's doing and to make sure it doesn't burn. Once one side is done, flip the foil packet over and repeat on the other side.

Boom! Grilled cheese sandwich! Adjust the toast level to your personal preference.

There you go — the perfect accompaniment to your late night study sessions. You can also add turkey or ham to make the sandwich heartier.

IRON-MADE BACON

Not only can you add turkey or ham to your grilled cheese, you can also add some…bacon! Here's how:

What you need: bacon, foil, towel, and iron.

- Tear a strip of bacon in half (you can make more or less depending on the size/width of your iron), and place on foil.
- Wrap in foil and crimp the sides — you don't want any bacon grease to escape.
- Set iron packet on a towel and place iron on top. Let it sit there for about 5 minutes, check to see how it is doing, and then flip and repeat. Again, cook time will depend on the heat of your iron and desired doneness of the bacon.
- Be careful when you open the foil — it's hot.

And there you have it. Freshly cooked bacon! In your dorm room! Made with an iron!

Okay, cooking with an iron isn't too practical, but it's really quite simple and fun. Give it a try — your lady friend or roommate will be delighted to know a real "iron chef!" Yar yar yar!

DAY 22

*How to
Make Small Talk*

—◆—

Are you already kind of dreading meeting your freshman dorm roommate for the first time, wondering what you're going to say?

When you spot an acquaintance in a store, do you hope they don't see you, pretend you don't see them, and try to covertly duck into another aisle?

Does the idea of walking into a party where you only know one person fill you with dread?

Do you keep trying to summon up the courage to talk to the cute girl who makes your lattes at the local coffee shop, but whenever you get up to the counter, all you can muster is your order?

When you're assigned to a table filled mostly with strangers at a wedding, do you talk only with your date, or sit hunched over your phone all night?

In this chapter we want to discuss the little dance you have to do before you get to plunge into that deeper level of communication: small talk. Small talk is the back and forth you have with strangers and acquaintances and even family members that you rarely see.

I wanted to cover this topic as part of this book because I have interacted with a lot of young men who couldn't engage in small talk to save their lives – really nice, earnest guys all, but their interactions with those beyond their circle of friends was painfully awkward. And while this form of communication may be "small," it's really a big deal when it comes to your personal and professional success, and your overall happiness. So before we discuss how to make it (and learn three, count 'em three, handy acronyms to improve your conversational skillz), let's talk about why it's so crucial.

Why the Ability to Make Small Talk Is So Important

It's easy to dismiss small talk as idle chit-chat, or superficial or pointless, and claim to only be interested in "real" conversation. But how do you get to the point of having a deeper conversation with someone in the first place? Someone you just met would be weirded out if you just walked up to them and asked, "Why do you think God allows bad things to happen to good people?" Conversation is a ladder, with small talk serving as the first few rungs. You can't leap-frog up the ladder. That would be like trying to sprint before warming up, or cook a steak without defrosting it, or merge onto a highway without building up speed on the on-ramp, or…well you get the idea.

Think about it. How did all of your current most important non-familial relationships begin? Most likely with a bit of small talk one day. Asking about a homework assignment in chemistry class or commiserating about the pain you were in while doing bear crawls down the football field. And now you're best buds.

Small talk is the portal through which every person you ever meet will enter your life. That's huge when you ponder it. You never know who you're going to encounter in a class, at a coffee shop, at the gym, at a wedding; they could be your future business partner or boss, your future best friend or wife. You simply never know when someone you meet will send your life in a new direction. But if you can't initiate these relationships, your circle of contacts and intimates will never expand past the current roster of friends whose Facebook updates and tweets you can't take your eyes off of in order to meet the gaze of those sitting right next to you.

How to Gain the Ability to Make Small Talk with Anyone, Anywhere

The first step in becoming an expert small talker is to start seeing yourself as the host, as opposed to the guest, in any situation. The host acts as a leader. He's active, not passive, and takes the initiative in talking with people, guiding the conversation, filling in awkward pauses, introducing people, and making others feel comfortable and welcome.

How do you become the consummate host wherever you go? Your hosting duties can be broken down into two categories: approaching others and being approachable.

How to Approach Others

Initiating Conversation with Strangers

We often feel self-conscious engaging a stranger in small talk, but most people are feeling as shy and insecure as you are. It's a great comfort and relief when someone takes the initiative to talk to them, saving them from standing alone by the punch bowl while they feel awkward and conspicuous. People love to talk (especially about themselves), and are typically flattered when someone is paying attention to them.

Look for someone who seems approachable, who's by himself, and isn't talking to someone else or working on something. Make eye contact, smile at them, and then go up to greet them.

But what then? Anyone who's had their small talk disintegrate after an exchange of "What do you do?" may worry that their attempt to initiate conservation will fizzle into awkwardness. But when you know what you're doing, you can sail right over any potential slumps.

The ARE method of initiating small talk. Communications expert Dr. Carol Fleming offers a three-part process to kick off a conversation: Anchor, Reveal, Encourage (ARE).

Anchor. This is an observation on your "mutual shared reality" that extends the first little thread of connection between you and another person — the lightest of pleasantries about something you're both seeing or experiencing.
- Dr. Landis is hilarious.
- The set list tonight has been fantastic.
- This weather is perfect.

Don't get caught up thinking that such comments are too superficial, and search in vain for something truly clever to say. Fleming calls such exchanges "friendly noises," and you both know they're not meaningful, but just a gradual and polite way to segue into a "real" conversation.

Reveal. Next, disclose something about yourself that is related to the anchor you just threw out.
- I've tried to get into Dr. Landis' class for three semesters, and this is the first time I was able to land a spot.
- There's a much bigger crowd here than there was at their show last year.

- I've been waiting for a break in the heat to go hike Mt. Whilston for the first time.

By opening up a little more, we extend to the other person a few more threads of connection and trust, while at the same time providing them fodder to which to respond.

Encourage. Now you hand the ball off to them by asking a question:
- Did you have a hard time getting into the class?
- Did you see that show?
- Have you ever done that hike?

Keep building the conversation. By employing the effective ARE method, you'll successfully have exchanged a few pleasantries, but these tender threads of small talk can easily disintegrate and blow away at this point…when the dreaded awkward pause shows up.

So you want to weave those light threads into an increasingly sturdy rope. You do this by offering follow-up comments and questions that continue to build the conversation. Let's take a look at how our three example conversations might progress:

> *You:* Dr. Landis is hilarious. I've tried to get into his class for three semesters and this is the first time I was able to land a spot. Did you have a hard time getting into the class?
> *Person:* Yeah, I actually sat on the stairs for the first few classes, and just hoped some people would drop out. Luckily they did, and he added me.

Once the person has answered your initial question, you can use a follow-up comment or question – each designed to prompt a response. Giving a comment takes more skill, as you have to craft one that will continue the back and forth. Ideally, you should form both a comment and a back-up question in your mind so that if they respond with only a laugh or an uh-huh, you're ready to get things moving again.

A clever/humorous comment is one option for your follow-up:

You (said jokingly): I'm thinking you had something to do with their disappearance!
Person (laughs): Oh, for sure! I tell ya, people are dying to get in here.
You: Are you taking this class for your major or just because you want to?

—

You: The set list tonight has been fantastic. There's a much bigger crowd here than at their show last year. Did you see that one?
Person: No, I didn't actually discover this band until a few weeks ago.

There's no good comment to give here that would keep the conversation going, so a follow-up question is most appropriate.

You: Oh yeah? How did you find out about them?

> *You*: This weather is perfect. I've been waiting for a break in the heat to hike Mt. Wilston. Have you ever done that hike?
>
> *Person*: No, I haven't.

Instead of being clever, another option for your follow-up comment is to share a little more about yourself.

> *You*: It's one of my favorite hikes. It only takes about an hour and a half to get to the top from the trailhead and the view is awesome.
>
> *Person*: Well the most I've hiked is up the hill on campus, but that does sound pretty doable.
>
> *You*: I think me and a couple of friends will be doing it tomorrow. If you're interested in coming along, let me know. I'm in 3B.

Whether you follow-up with a comment or question, be sure to alternate between the two options. Strike a balance; too many questions fired one right after the other will make the conversation feel more like an interrogation, and too many comments won't give the other person a chance to talk; that's no good, as your interest in what they have to say is what endears you to them.

So tip the scale more heavily towards questions. Once they respond to one question, you ask clarifying questions about their answer. Start with questions that can be answered with one or two words, and then build on those to expand into open-ended questions that won't put them on the spot, but will allow them to reveal more or less about themselves, depending on their comfort level. Use questions that begin with phrases like:

- Tell me about…
- What was the best part of…
- How did you feel about…
- What brought you to…
- What's surprised you most…
- How similar/different is that to…
- Why…

Here are some effective small talk chains, with the common, but less open-ended questions marked through, and a better alternative following it:

- Where are you from? → ~~Did you live there all of your life?~~ What was it like to grow up there? → What brought you here? → Are any of your family members close by? → ~~How many siblings do you have?~~ Tell me more about your family. → Is it tough being away from them? → What do you miss most about your hometown?
- What are you majoring in? → What made you decide to choose that major? → ~~How do you like it?~~ What's been the best class you've taken so far? → Tell me more about it. → What was the most interesting part of the class? → Do you think you might write about that for your thesis?
- What do you do? → ~~Do you like your job?~~ Describe a

typical day at work. → How has the economy affected business? → Why has your company thrived while others have taken a beating? → Would you recommend a young man like myself going into the field? → Do you know anyone who might be looking for an intern?

INITIATING CONVERSATION WITH ACQUAINTANCES

Starting some small talk with an acquaintance – someone you only chat with a bit at church each Sunday, a coworker you see around the office sometimes, an old friend you don't keep in very good contact with but run into occasionally – requires a different approach than breaking the ice with a stranger. In an encounter with an acquaintance, you'll likely start with a question, but how you craft that question is important.

Ask open-ended questions. Here's how it usually goes: How was your weekend? How's your day going? How have you been? Whatadya been up to? Fine. Fine. Good. Not much… cue the crickets! Questions like these are conversation killers — they only prompt a one or two-word response, and are basically used by most people as rote hellos in passing, not as questions where an actual answer is expected.

So you have to follow up:

- How was your weekend? Good. What did you do?
- How's your day going? Good. What's been the best part so far?
- How have you been? Good. What's been going well for you?

If the acquaintance gives another abbreviated response, you can say something like, "What else? I really want to know." People are used to going through the motions with folks, and are looking for permission to talk a little about themselves. But if they remain reticent, they may simply not want to talk, and you should always respect that.

Catching up with an acquaintance has unique pitfalls: you know only an outline of his life, but you don't know what's changed in it since the last time you talked. So you want to frame your questions with care and keep them neutral to avoid "stepping in it":

- ~~Have you landed a job yet?~~ (turns out he's still unemployed) → What's been going on with the job search lately?
- ~~How's Jen?~~ (she just dumped him) → Bring me up to date about you and Jen.
- ~~I heard you took a trip out to Cali last month. That must have been awesome!~~ (he had to go to California because his dad died) → What brought you out to California last month?
- ~~How long have you two been dating?~~ (they haven't discussed whether they are actually dating yet) → How did you two meet?

WHAT DO I DO IF I HAVE TROUBLE COMING UP WITH QUESTIONS OR THINGS TO SAY?

Observe. Some of the easiest and best questions simply come from observing people and their surroundings:

- I see you got your Ph.D from the University of Washington. Why did you pick that school?
- Ah, you're reading *The Great Gatsby*? That's my favorite book. How are you liking it?

- I can't help but notice you're a fan of the Jets. Who do you think their starting QB is going to be?
- Tell me about this picture. Are you running a marathon? Who's running with you?
- How do you like your Jeep Wrangler?
- Where did you get your hair cut? I'm looking for a good barber.

Listen. You can start a conversation by building on something someone said that wasn't directly addressed to you, but you were privy to.

For example, in smaller classes in college, sometimes the professor will have everyone introduce themselves on the first day of class. If there's someone in the class you'd like to get to know more, you can later start a conversation by saying something like: "You mentioned you were from Colorado. What part?"

Or after a business presentation, go up to the speaker and say: "I thought you made an interesting point about the benefits the traditional newspaper offers over the online version. What do you think is the future of print?"

Compliment. A good way to kick off some small talk is to tie a compliment and a question together:
- That's a really nice fountain pen. Is it hard to learn to write with one?
- I was really impressed with the patience you showed with those kids today. How do you stay so calm when they're bouncing off the walls?

When complimenting a woman, stick with a behavior, accomplishment, or article of clothing rather than a body part.

FORM a question in your mind. If you're at a table with a group of people and the small talk hits a snag, remember the acronym FORM:

- **Family.** Tell me about your family. Are your siblings alike or different? What new things is your kid doing these days? How's your grandpa's health?
- **Occupation.** What are the best and worst parts of your job? How has the economy affected your industry?
- **Recreation.** Are you still running these days? Have you gone on any camping trips lately? What's the latest thing you've built in your workshop? Seen any good movies lately? Read any good books?
- **Motivation.** Where do you hope to be in five years? Do you find your job satisfying? What do you like about your new church?

MAKE YOURSELF APPROACHABLE

It's true what Dale Carnegie said: "You can make more friends in two months by becoming interested in other people than you can in two years trying to get other people interested in you."

But it's also nice when others initiate the conversation. Sometimes you're just not in "host" mode and raring to initiate conversation, but you're still open for small talk. If you want strangers to strike up a conversation with you, you need to put out the vibe that you're open to it and that you'd be an interesting person to talk with. You need to be approachable.

In figuring out how to be a more approachable, just take a look around the room. What people attract you, and which do you seek to avoid. What does each set do or neglect to do?

Wear a conversation piece. People often feel the most comfortable in approaching you to ask about some specific item you're wearing. An arrestingly handsome tie (not a novelty tie), an interesting tie tack, a lapel pin, a unique (but tasteful) ring, watch, or necklace, even a printed t-shirt (I'm not talking Affliction here, you know…let's say one with "Semper Virilis" on it, for example) worn in a casual setting, can all easily inspire curious questions that spark a conversation.

Exhibit friendly body language. Our nonverbal body language accounts for the majority of how others perceive us. Body language that is warm and inviting will draw others to you and make them feel comfortable conversing.

Arthur Wassmer came up with the last acronym we'll cover today — SOFTEN — to describe the elements of nonverbal behavior that attract others:

- **Smile.** A warm, friendly smile puts others at ease. When you're walking around, display a slight, soft smile. After you make eye contact with someone, give them a bigger, genuine smile.
- **Open** posture. Instead of standing at an angle, with your arms crossed or in your pockets, face others directly and hang your arms naturally by your sides.

- **Forward** lean. When listening or speaking, leaning in shows someone you are paying attention. The more intimacy you build with someone, the closer you can lean, but at first, respect the person's physical space.
- **Touch** by shaking hands. A good hearty handshake, where the web between your thumb and pointer finger meets theirs, conveys confidence and vitality.
- **Eye** contact. Being able to make eye contact shows you're confident and builds intimacy with others.
- **Nod.** Whenever you listen to someone speak, nodding, along with other verbal and nonverbal forms of feedback like "uh-huhs" and "hmmms," show you're focused on what the speaker has to say.

Be well-groomed and well-dressed. Not over-dressed – that will drive folks away and make you seem uptight. But don some clean clothes that fit well and exhibit your own style and lots of confidence.

And a note about facial hair...it's a dynamo conversation starter. Everyone wants to comment on my mustache. And beards, while they used to be the mark of the crusty backwoodsman or shifty rebel, are now often read by folks as "approachable" – the look of a super laid-back, good-humored guy.

Offer your name to those you've met before. A new acquaintance may not remember it. A former professor may have had thousands of students come through their classes. Trying to figure out your name as you talk, along with the worry that the fact they don't know it will be revealed, will distract them from focusing on the conversation. So just offer it up when you see them: "Hi, Dr. Smith, Brett McKay from last year's History 101!"

Never give one word answers. A "yes," or "no" FULL STOP sounds curt. Ever been to this event before? No. Are you a friend of the groom? Yes. Just add a bit to soften it, as it makes you sound more game to talk: *No I haven't. Yes I am.*

Expand your answers, even when a "No I haven't" or "Yes I am" will technically suffice. Examples: "No I haven't, but my friend Michael Davidson finally convinced me to come this year. Do you know him? I think you guys went to the same high school." Or: "Yes I am. Chuck and I were fraternity brothers at the University of Alabama."

The goal here is to provide your small talk partner with more information from which they can make a comment or pose a question that will keep the conversation going. Just think of when the shoe's on the other foot – the more fodder someone gives you, the easier it is to formulate a good response.

Mirror your partner. People feel more comfortable, and are charmed more, by those who match their behavior, tone of voice, talking speed, and so on. Don't match your conversation partner tic for tic, but if they speak softly, bring your own voice down a notch; if they're enthusiastic, act similarly.

Give an accessible description of your job. One of the most common questions for folks to ask is, "What do you do?"

If your job is pretty technical, try to put it in layman's terms so that they have something to ask you follow-up questions about, as opposed to just saying, "Oh, nuclear fission, huh?"

Have a wide range of knowledge and keep up with current events. By being well-read and keeping up with what's going on in the world, you'll always have a bit of knowledge to match the varied interests of those you meet.

PRACTICE!

Technology has created an interesting phenomenon in which people increasingly crave real face-to-face connection, while at the same time becoming less equipped to facilitate it.

The only way to get better at small talk is to practice. And you have to practice it in situations where it really doesn't matter, so that you're ready when it does.

Strike up some small talk with the man behind the deli counter or the person working the register at the grocery store: How's your day going? How much longer on your shift? What's been the best part of your day so far?

Instead of ducking out of events that you're not too keen on attending, go with the express purpose of practicing your small talk skills. Look it as your conversation lab – you don't care much about what the people there think of you anyway, so feel free to try things out and make mistakes.

Don't get hung up on "failing." If someone's not interested in talking, that's okay. No harm, no foul; just move on. Small talk is only annoying when it's unwelcome, and the initiator fails to pick up on this disinterest. If the person you're trying to engage gives several short answers, and keeps angling their body away from you, let them get on with whatever they'd rather be doing.

But as the old saying goes, you have to wrestle some gators to make a gator soup. All experiences, good and bad, will help you hone your mastery of small talk, so you can talk to that girl on the shuttle to campus with ease, and you don't have to wait in your car to avoid walking up the stairs to your apartment at the same time as someone else.

Sources:
It's the Way You Say It by Carol Fleming
The Fine Art of Small Talk by Debra Fine
Talk to Strangers by David Topus
Ye Olde Book of Life Experience

DAY 23

How to Iron
a Dress Shirt

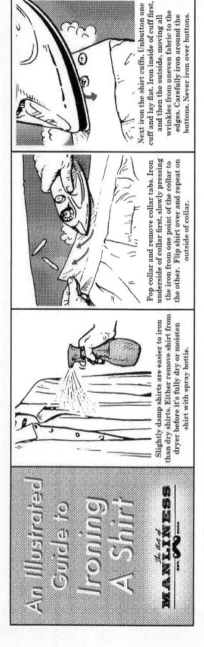

An Illustrated Guide to Ironing A Shirt

The Art of MANLINESS

Slightly damp shirts are easier to iron than dry shirts. Either remove shirt from dryer before it's fully dry or moisten shirt with spray bottle.

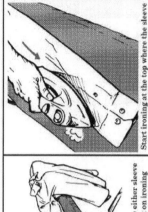

Next iron the shirt cuffs. Unbutton one cuff and lay flat. Iron inside of cuff first, and then the outside, moving all wrinkles from uneven fabric to the edges. Carefully iron around the buttons. Never iron over buttons.

Pop collar and remove collar tabs. Iron underside of collar first, slowly pressing the iron from one point of the collar to the other. Flip shirt over and repeat on outside of collar.

Start ironing at the top where the sleeve is sewn onto the shirt and work your way down to the cuff. Turn sleeve over and iron the opposite side, then repeat process with other sleeve.

Time for the sleeves. Take either sleeve by the seam and lay flat on ironing board. If you can see the crease on the top of the sleeve from previous ironing, match it again so that you have a single crease line.

Iron back of shirt. Start at the top with the yoke (back shoulder area) and slowly slide the iron down. If you have a center box pleat, spend a few seconds ironing around it.

Iron front of shirt. Start with the side with buttons and carefully work the iron point around button area. Then move back up to the top of the shoulder and work your way down the shirt with iron. Repeat on other side.

DAY 24

How to be a
Savvy Consumer

As men, we should strive to create more, and consume less. But less doesn't mean nothing. You're going to spend most of your life as a consumer of goods and services like cars, clothes, healthcare, and even your education.

Never in human history have there been so many choices as to what to spend your money on. And never have marketing tactics to get you to buy those things been so sophisticated. Every time you swipe a store loyalty card, use your smartphone, log into Facebook, or surf the net, companies are mining this data, gathering information on your address, family size, education and income level, favorite books, movies, and hobbies, and history of purchasing behavior. This data is then fed into complex algorithms that craft ways to target you with ads and mailings pitched to your specific hopes, dreams, and insecurities. Corporations have you in their sights.

Now, I don't want to paint too sinister a face on it – companies are simply offering products and services that people want – but to the degree that marketers track you, they are essentially "predators" on the hunt. They don't want to eat you, certainly (you're much more valuable alive!), they just want to burrow into your mind and get you to buy their stuff. They've got millions of dollars and sophisticated tools at their disposal, so the playing field is far from level, but as the "prey," you can definitely put up a fight. You need to be educated and empowered — an informed, savvy consumer who doesn't buy mindlessly on impulse and end up with a house full of useless or non-functioning junk and a mountain of debt. The savvy consumer makes his purchases on his terms and does his homework to make sure he doesn't get ripped off, receives the most bang for his buck, and only buys what he truly wants and needs.

UNDERSTAND THE PRINCIPLE OF VALUE VS. PRICE

A few years ago, we did a project where we asked AoM readers to write up "Lessons in Manliness" profiles on the ordinary men in our lives, describing how these mentors embodied manliness and inspired us.

Something that I remember really striking me at the time was how many of the profiles mentioned that the man in question always made purchases based on the quality of a product rather than simply its price. When making a purchasing decision, they looked for things that would last.

My grandfather was this kind of savvy consumer, and yours probably was (or is) too. He 1) didn't care about amassing a lot of possessions, but wanted the possessions he did have to do their job and bring him enjoyment, and 2) he understood that just because something was cheap, didn't make it a bargain. To figure out the true value of something, he looked beyond the sticker price, to the price per use.

GAUGING PRICE PER USE

Let's start with the example of a leather briefcase. Bob shops on price and buys a nylon messenger bag for $50. Frank, however, buys a leather briefcase with a lifetime warranty for $500. They each use their respective bags 200 times a year. Bob's cheap bag wears out after three years and he has to replace it.

Frank's leather bag lasts 50 years, and he hands it down to his grandson. In Bob's case the price per use on his bag was about 8 cents (200 uses a year X 3 years divided into $50). For Frank, his cost per use was 5 cents, which will only go down as his grandson continues to use the bag. So ultimately, while Bob's bag was initially a whole lot cheaper, in the long run Frank's purchase will turn out to be the better deal.

Something that will also affect this equation is how often you use the product. As Darren Bush – owner of an outdoors store and regular AoM contributor – points out, if someone tries to save money by buying equipment over the internet, and that equipment ends up not fitting right, it will sit in the garage gathering dust, and its cost per use will soar. If the same person had gone to their local mom and pop store, where a trained salesperson helped them pick out just the right item, one they used as much as possible and got years of enjoyment out of, the cost per use plummets, making the more expensive purchase the true bargain over time.

Another good example of this is buying a mattress — you'll be spending a third of your life on it, so purchasing one that helps you get a deep sleep night after night is an incredible value, even if the mattress you choose is more expensive than a cheaper model that would have left you tossing and turning just to save a few bucks up front.

Generic versus Brand Name

Of course, when determining price versus value, always look into what you're getting for the higher price. It can equate to higher quality, but certainly not always. The high price might simply go to support a brand name, a celebrity endorsement, or a big advertising budget. This is why when it comes to buying generic items over brand name ones, you have to experiment to find out what the extra cost of the well-known brand is netting you. Some generic brands are actually made in the same factory as the brand name ones, while some are cheaper because of their inferior quality. Here are a few examples:

At the grocery store:
- Cheaper paper towels and toilet paper — you often end up having to use more sheets to get the job done. Doesn't always pay to go cheap here.
- Garbage bags — lift a cheap packed-to-the-max bag out of the can and be prepared to watch the bottom fall out. You only want to experience this once.
- Generic zip lock bags — more than adequate as they seal fine and in all probability will only be used once anyway.
- Sugar is sugar and salt is salt.
- Medicines — the FDA requires that the active ingredient in generic medicines be the same as brand name versions. So a generic headache medicine will work just as well as Tylenol.

In the hardware store:
- Paint brushes — buy the best you can. They will hold more paint, be easier to work with, and last you a long time. You never want to try to draw a fine bead of paint with a junky brush that has the bristles splayed in every direction.
- Paint — when you have to apply a second coat of paint because the first didn't hide the original color, you'll rue

your decision to save a few bucks per gallon.

- Drill bits — cheap ones snap or quickly become dull, resulting in your schlepping back to Home Depot in order to finish drilling the last 3/8″ hole in your project. Alas, this is harder to realize now that almost all, if not all, drill bits come from China.

It's hard to know whether a generic item will be as good as a brand name without trying it out. That works for garbage bags, but of course you don't want to experiment and get burned when you're buying a big-ticket item. We'll cover how to carefully make those higher-end purchases below.

Don't Be Dazzled by Features

Marketing expert Martin Lindstrom says that while men believe they don't let their feelings get in the way of their purchasing decisions, their shopping behavior is best defined as "emorational." Women do make more emotional purchases than men in general, but men often disguise their emotional impulse to buy by concentrating on the practical features of a product. Men like to learn about something's specs, and can rationalize that getting a more expensive product with a ton of features makes sense. In reality, it's often the coolness of the product — the way he imagines owning it will make him feel — that is luring him. Paying a hundred dollars more for something with twelve features when you only need two isn't a good value.

Of course when you're first starting out in life, you often can't afford the higher upfront costs of quality products, and you shouldn't go into debt to get them. Try to make your cheaper products last as long as possible; don't buy a replacement if it's not broken, and try to fix it to extend its life. The longer you use it, the more time you'll have to save up for a quality item that will last.

To sum up: instead of purchasing a lot of crap, a savvy consumer gets a few good things that will bring him a lifetime of utility and enjoyment.

RESEARCH, RESEARCH, RESEARCH

Before making any big purchase or contracting a service, a savvy consumer does as much research as they can. Your goal is to find out if the product will give you the most bang for your buck and will satisfy your demands for quality and safety. If you're buying a product, just Google the name of it, as specifically as you can, plus "review." If you're buying an appliance, try hopping on Amazon or BestBuy.com and read the reviews there. For electronics, *cnet.com* is the place to go. You'll need to use your discernment and have some patience with reviews offered by the public; up to 30% of the reviews may be fake — created by the company that makes the product or the guy who offers the service. Also keep in mind that people who were unhappy are more likely to leave a review than those who were pleased. I like to read a few reviews in the highest, lowest, and in-between categories and then kind of average them together in my mind to get an overall feel for how the product most likely really is.

There are also sites and publications that offer reviews for specific products. For example, *Edmunds.com* and Car and Driver are great for researching vehicle purchases.

It might even be worth it in some cases to pay for one

month's access to Consumer Reports online reviews. I've done this when buying things like computers and washers/dryers.

When shopping for a specific brand name item, use Google Shopping to find the lowest price, then use Bizrate.com to check on the merchant's reputation. It is not worth saving a few dollars if you end up hassling with a sleazy vendor.

If you're researching a service provider, Angie's List is the way to go. Look for someone who gets high marks on quality, reliability, and price. It also doesn't hurt to ask your friends, family, and co-workers for recommendations too. In many cases, posing a question on Facebook to your local friends and family about reliable providers will net you better results than any search engine could.

GET PRICE QUOTES FROM SEVERAL BUSINESSES BEFORE MAKING A PURCHASE

When it comes to hiring someone to perform a service, it really pays to shop around, as prices can vary widely. Again, a lower price may mean lower quality, while at the same time you don't want to assume that if something is more expensive, it's automatically better.

Getting multiple quotes allows you to make service providers compete against each other. If there's a guy you want to use for various reasons, but another guy gives you a lower price, you can always go back to the first guy and say, "This is guy's willing to do it for X, can you match that price?"

Yes, shopping around does take a bit of extra time, but it's totally worth it if it means you can save hundreds or even thousands of dollars.

Learn How to Negotiate

For most young men in America, negotiating is a completely foreign concept. We're socialized into thinking that you simply pay the price offered and that it's rude to haggle. But if you want your dollar to go as far as it can, you need to learn how to negotiate. This skill can save you a ton of money over your lifetime. Is staying in your comfort zone really worth thousands of dollars that you basically threw out the window?

Some of your biggest purchases in your life will require you to negotiate — cars and homes being the most obvious. But even if you're not in the market yet for these big-ticket items, knowing how to negotiate can still serve you well. Everything from your car insurance rate to your gym membership is negotiable.

Last year, Tyler Tervooren wrote an amazingly comprehensive guide to haggling for us. I highly recommend giving it a read: *www.artofmanliness.com/2011/05/11/how-to-haggle-like-your-old-man*. Also, check out *Getting to Yes* by Roger Fisher and William Ury — the book is crammed with tips on how to negotiate like a pro.

Ignore Up-Sales

When you walk into a store or even shop online, businesses want you to spend more money than you originally planned on. To encourage you to open your wallet, they use a technique called up-selling. Up-selling means suggesting upgrades, add-ons, and additional services to customers right before they pay for their original purchase. It's amazingly effective when done right. Studies show that sales can increase by as much as 40% simply by implementing up-selling at the point of purchase.

You encounter up-selling all the time, but may not have known what it was called. It's especially common practice at restaurants. After she brings out your drinks, the waitress will probably say something like, "Would you gentlemen like to try to some of our amazing fried pickles as an appetizer?" You just got up-sold.

Whenever you shop on Amazon.com, you probably see a list of items that other customers bought who also bought the book you're buying. That's another example of up-selling.

Those types of up-sells are rather benign and can actually be useful. I can't count the number of times I discovered a fantastic book thanks to Amazon's suggestions. But you don't want to be lured into buying something you don't need or don't have the money for.

The up-sells savvy consumers really need to watch for occur when you buy large appliances or computers.

Think back to the last time you bought a computer or some other expensive gizmo. You've got the product at the checkout counter and before the clerk rings you up he asks, "Would you like to buy an extended warranty? It's only $25 and it will protect you even if you throw your laptop into a volcano as some sort of sacrifice." As a general rule, a savvy consumer should decline most extended warranty offers. You probably won't need it; the manufacturer's warranty is usually sufficient. Companies know the chances that you'll actually use the warranty are slim, which is why they push them so hard. In fact, more than 80% of extended warranties go unused. So if a company can sell you one, it's often pure profit for them.

Also, watch out for up-sells in the form of add-ons you really don't need. For example, whenever you buy an HDTV, you'll probably be told by the guy at Best Buy that you need to get some special $75 HDTV surge protector as well as diamond encased HDMI cables to ensure the best possible resolution. According to my brother, who once worked at Best Buy, you should always, always say no to this stuff. "They don't do anything. The profit margins on them are high. That's why we're told to recommend them," he says.

Bottom line: know exactly what you want before making a purchase, and don't give in to high-pressure up-sells.

READ CONTRACTS BEFORE SIGNING

Renting an apartment, joining a gym, getting cell phone service, and purchasing health insurance are just a few of the services and products that require us to sign a contract. These agreements legally obligate you and the other party to fulfill certain terms. Failing to stick to your end of the contract can result in stiff penalties and possibly a lawsuit. That's why it's so important to take the time to thoroughly read a contract before you sign your name on the dotted line.

Unfortunately, many people don't even bother to read contracts because they are long and sometimes overwhelming. While it's a pain in the rear, get in the habit of reading all contracts before you sign them. If you have to, take it home and read it when you have more time. While you're reading, look for the following things:

- How much and when will you pay?
- How long does the contract last?
- What are the penalties and consequences if one side doesn't stick to the agreement?
- How does the contract end? Is there an auto-renewal? And if so, how can you stop it if you no longer want the service?
- What are the causes of terminating the contract?
- How are contract disputes resolved? Arbitration? Mediation? Courts?
- Are all the blanks filled in? Oftentimes contracts will have blank spaces where prices and dates are filled in. Make sure those spaces are filled in before signing so that someone can't make any changes without your knowledge.
- Are all the oral and handshake agreements written in the contract?

Don't be afraid to ask any questions. Also, if you find any terms that you don't agree with, ask that they be changed. Before you sign, any of the terms in the contract are negotiable.

After you sign the contract, make sure you get copies of it for your records, which brings us to…

KEEP YOUR RECEIPTS, AGREEMENTS, CONTRACTS, ETC.

Before you purchase something, you should always find out exactly what the store's return policy is, and after your purchase, you need to hold onto your receipt. If you ever have a problem with a product or service and want to make a return or complaint, you'll need it, along with any contracts you may have signed. So get in the habit of putting your receipts and agreements in a folder for safekeeping. Never again will you have to rummage through your car or random drawers looking for the receipt for your defunct TV.

Better yet, digitize all your receipts and contracts and store them in the cloud. I'm slowly making this a habit. I'm using the Evernote app on my iPhone to quickly snap photos of receipts and tagging them with "receipt." I scan large documents like contracts directly into Evernote on my laptop. Now I don't have to worry about misplacing receipts, and I have access to them anytime and anywhere.

DAY 25

Establish an
Exercise Routine

———•———

When I was in high school, I didn't have to worry about creating and sticking to a fitness routine. I had football coaches who took care of that for me. I just had to show up at the weight room at the designated time with the rest of my teammates and do the scheduled workout. Because of that consistency, along with a lot of hard work, I was in really good shape when I graduated and headed off to college.

With my football days behind me, I pretty much stopped working out once I arrived on campus. I'd play the occasional pick-up basketball game, but I didn't have a set fitness routine to maintain the strength and conditioning I achieved while in high school. Boy, did things deteriorate quickly for me. I started to get soft and pudgy and my strength was nowhere near the levels I was used to. I remember one night during my freshman year in college I decided to go to the gym in an attempt to get back on track. I slapped 225 lbs on the bench barbell to start off. It was a weight I had easily lifted in high school. I lifted the barbell off the rack and began to slowly lower it to my chest...where it stayed until my cries of help were heard. Thankfully, only my ego was bruised. But that moment really spurred me to get back on the fitness bandwagon.

I've noticed that a lot of young men heading out on their own fall into the same trap I did. Sometimes they were physically active in high school because of sports, but as soon as they head off to college they stop exercising completely and quickly become the stereotypical fat ex-jock. Don't let this happen to you! It's harder to get back into shape once you've gotten flabby than it is to maintain the shape you're already in. That's why it's so important you keep a regular exercise routine when you head out on your own.

If you didn't exercise regularly in high school, without working out (and a healthy diet) you won't become a fat ex-jock, you'll just become fat. Plenty of guys who maintained an average weight in college find themselves growing a belly as they move into their mid and late 20s — a diet of fast food and plenty of beer takes its toll.

When I went with Kate to her ten-year high school reunion, I was struck by the fact that while most of the women seemed to have maintained their figures (despite some of them having children), the dudes looked pretty out of shape and overweight.

The first few years living out on your own will a build a foundation for the rest of your life, so unless you want to become the middle-aged guy who gets all wheezy when playing with his kids, now is the time to establish a fitness routine for yourself.

Why You Need a Fitness Routine

Increases testosterone. Testosterone is what makes men, men. Unfortunately, most young men have lower testosterone than their grandfathers did because of changes in diet, activity levels, and chemicals in our environment, water, and food supply. The benefits of optimal testosterone levels are numerous. Besides increasing your libido, testosterone does the following:

- Increases mental and physical energy
- Boosts happiness (men with low T often suffer depression)
- Increases competitive drive

- Helps prevent Alzheimer's and dementia
- Increases muscle size and strength

Compound weightlifting exercises like squats, bench presses, cleans, and deadlifts are great testosterone boosters. High intensity exercises, like sprinting, have been shown to boost testosterone levels as well.

Good for your brain. If you want to be a stellar college student, you need to hit the treadmill in addition to hitting the books. Studies show that regular exercise speeds learning, improves memory, and promotes clearer thinking.

Increases your willpower. Willpower is an important factor in success for men. One way to strengthen it is to make regular exercise a habit. Working out will increase your discipline in all areas of your life.

Reduced health costs. Health costs are ballooning here in the U.S. because of the rise of obesity and obesity-related diseases like diabetes, heart disease, and hypertension. While proper diet plays the biggest role in preventing obesity, regular exercise can help stave off weight gain and improve how your body uses insulin so you don't get diabetes. A regular fitness routine has also been shown to reduce blood pressure and improve heart health. If you don't want to spend a small fortune treating these ailments in the future, get in the gym today. Not only will you reduce your own health care costs by being physically fit, you can take some manly pride knowing you're not increasing costs for your neighbors and fellow citizens.

Relieves stress and depression. We're going to go into more detail about managing stress later in the book, but one thing you can start doing today that will go a long way to keeping you chill like The Dude is to exercise. It releases endorphins in your brain, improves sleep, and can relieve feelings of anxiety and depression. Exercising regularly is truly one of the most important things you can do to stay sane during college.

Makes you physically attractive. Your physical attractiveness can play a big role in your personal and professional success. Women are more attracted to men who are fit and in shape. Men who are physically attractive often report higher incomes and more job promotions than men who are less attractive. Exercise can help mold a physique that will make you attractive to others, and even more importantly, boost your confidence in yourself.

ESTABLISHING AN EXERCISE ROUTINE

A lot of men know it's important to exercise, but end up feeling lost as to what to do for their workout. There are so many opinions out there as to what the "best" workout is that you can end up feeling overwhelmed and not doing anything at all. When I'd go to the gym at OU, I'd often see guys just kind of wandering around aimlessly, half-hardheartedly doing a few bicep curls and tricep extensions.

In truth, at least in my opinion, unless your fitness goal is to get super shredded or have a bodybuilder's physique, you shouldn't stress about finding the "perfect" workout. Instead, focus on improving your overall strength and fitness with a routine that's as simple as possible – one you will enjoy and do consistently. The most important thing is to do something, anything, to move your body every day!

Below I suggest two exercise routines that are perfect for a young man who is busy, but is looking to maximize results. One requires access to a gym and free-weights, while the other consists solely of bodyweight exercises.

StrongLifts 5x5 Workout

My favorite workout routine is the StrongLifts 5×5 (*stronglifts.com*) routine promoted by a guy named Mehdi in Belgium. It's fast (workouts take about 40 minutes), you don't need much equipment, it produces great results, and it's very doable for a beginner who's new to lifting. I also like it because it's similar to the strength training program I did as a high school football player. I'm stronger and leaner than I've ever been since starting Mehdi's StrongLifts program.

The program is simple. There are two workouts (A & B), each consisting of five exercises:

Workout A
- Squat (5 sets of 5 reps)
- Bench Press (5 sets of 5 reps)
- Inverted Rows (3 sets of as many reps as you can perform in each set until muscle failure)
- Push-ups (3 sets until failure)
- Reverse Crunch (3 sets of 12 reps)

Workout B

- Squat (5 sets of 5 reps)
- Overhead Press (5 sets of 5 reps)
- Deadlift (1 set of 5 reps)
- Pull-ups/Chin-ups (3 sets until failure)
- Prone Bridges (3 sets each set lasting 30 seconds)

You do 5 sets of 5 (1 set of 5 on the deadlift) using the same weight throughout the exercise, e.g., if your first set on the bench press is 135 lbs, your last set should be 135 lbs, too. I rest two minutes between each set.

Every other day, you alternate workout A & B. Once a week, give yourself a break from lifting for 48 hours.

So for example, my schedule using StrongLifts 5×5 looks like this:

- Monday: Workout A
- Tuesday: Sprints
- Wednesday: Workout B
- Thursday: Long-distance run
- Friday: Workout A
- Saturday: Rest (I usually take a nice walk)
- Sunday: Rest

The following week, I start off with workout B:

- Monday: Workout B
- Tuesday: Plyometrics
- Wednesday: Workout A
- Thursday: Long-distance run
- Friday: Workout B

- Saturday: Rest
- Sunday: Rest

Every workout, add 5 lbs to the weight you lifted in the previous session. If you ever reach a plateau, reduce your weight by 10% and start slowly adding 5 lbs again until you break through it.

That's the basics of the program. I highly recommend that you download Mehdi's free ebook from the website to get a more comprehensive and detailed look at the workout. The ebook includes links to instructions on how to do the exercises, some nice spreadsheets you can use to track your progress, and other helpful info on how to get started with StrongLifts 5×5. Also, take some time to peruse his website for even more information. (I have zero affiliation with Medhi, by the way; this is honestly the program I use myself and have gotten good results from.)

On the days I'm not doing the 5×5 program (Tuesdays and Thursdays), I do my cardio workouts:

- Tuesdays: Sprints or plyometrics. For my sprint workouts I go to the middle school football field near my house and mark off 40 yards with some cones. I'll warm up with a jog around the football field with some dynamic warm-ups mixed in. I'll then do 40 sets of full-out 40-yard sprints, resting about a minute between each sprint. I'm starting to add one sprint to every workout. This is High Intensity Training (HIT), which is super effective at boosting your aerobic capacity, lowering blood sugar levels, and burning fat. For my plyometrics workout I follow the program I wrote

about a few years ago: *www.artofmanliness.com/2010/05/21/
beginners-guide-to-plyometrics*
- Thursdays: Long-distance run (well, long distance for me).
I usually do a 5k, and I use the NikeRun app to track my
progress. I make sure my course has some challenging hills.

BODYWEIGHT WORKOUT

This bodyweight program is one I do sometimes when I
can't or don't want to go to the gym. It works your entire body
and can be done anywhere. The only equipment this routine
requires is an Iron Gym Pull-Up Bar that you can place in any
doorframe and which doesn't require you to drill any holes. Even
if you plan on going to the gym regularly, buying an Iron Gym
Pull-Up Bar is a great investment for any young man. Make it
a policy to crank out a few pull-ups each time you pass through
the doorframe from which it hangs.

Even if you can't swing an Iron Gym bar, I'm sure you could
find a tree branch or another bar that could be used for pull-ups.

This is a circuit program, meaning you do each of the exer-
cises back-to-back without any rest. When you've completed
all the exercises, you've completed one circuit. If you aren't
familiar with any of the exercises, a quick YouTube search will
get you on track.
- **Squats:** 20 reps
- **Push-ups**: 10 reps
- **Hindu push-ups**: 10 reps
- **Walking Lunges**: 20 reps
- **Pull-ups**: 5 reps
- **Dips**: 15 reps

Do a ten-minute warm-up first (jumping jacks, jump rope, jogging), and then complete each exercise back-to-back without resting. That's a circuit. Rest for two minutes after completing a circuit and then start another one.

Start with one circuit, and then add a circuit once you're able to perform all the reps for all the exercises. Keep adding circuits until you can complete all the reps for all the exercises for five circuits. After that, start adding 1 rep to each exercise at each workout.

Perform this workout every other day, three times a week. Here's a suggested schedule:

- Monday: Bodyweight workout
- Tuesday: Sprints or plyometrics
- Wednesday: Bodyweight workout
- Thursday: 5K run
- Friday: Bodyweight workout
- Saturday: Rest
- Sunday: Rest

Whatever workout program you choose, the key is to be consistent with it. Treat your workouts like an important doctor's appointment. When you plan your week, block off a time each day for exercise.

You should also look for ways to incorporate exercise into your everyday life – walk and bike to campus when you can, join an intramural team, play some pick-up games of ultimate Frisbee with your buds, and take a date on a bike ride. Establishing a habit of regular exercise – both at the gym and throughout your day — will reap enormous benefits for the rest of your life.

DAY 26

15 Maxims
for Being a
Reliable Man

———◆———

As we head into our last week of this *Heading Out on Your Own* book, I'd like to pause from our "harder," more practical skills to talk about a character trait, that, like self-reliance, is both an important building block in your life's foundation, and, unfortunately, too often in short supply amongst young men.

Being reliable.

The word reliable has its origins in *relier*, Old French for "fasten" or "attach"; the reliable man was an immovable pillar of strength on which you could hang your hat, someone you could lean and depend on, a man you could trust.

Compare that image with its opposite: the flake. Floating, drifting, fragile; melting as soon as it meets any resistance.

We've all known reliable men, and we've all known flakes. We admire the former, and avoid the latter. To become the kind of man you've grown up trusting and counting on, read on.

WHY BE RELIABLE?

"Only recently a prominent public man was criticized throughout the newspaper world as one not having enough character to keep his promises. He had not the stamina to make good when to do so proved difficult. He hadn't the timber, the character fiber to stand up and do the thing he knew to be right, and that he had promised to do. The world is full of these jelly-fish people who have not lime enough in their backbone to stand erect, to do the right thing. They are always stepping into the spotlight in the good-intention stage, and then, when the reckoning time comes, taking the line of least resistance, doing the thing which will cost the

least effort or money, regardless of later consequences. They think they can be as unscrupulous about breaking promises as they were about making them. But sooner or later fate makes us play fair or get out of the game."
—Orison Swett Marden, *Making Life a Masterpiece*, 1916

The reliable man forges deeper relationships. Relationships are built on trust; without it they wither and die. Being reliable builds that trust – your friends and loved ones know that they can count on you to keep your word, be there when you'll say you'll be, and do what you say you'll do. They can also feel secure that you'll be the same man day after day, no matter what happens. That you won't be capricious with your warmth, blanketing them with affection one day and then withdrawing into prickly remoteness the next. That you won't sometimes be patient with their foibles, and other times fly into a rage at the slightest provocation. Without this steady reliability in your mood and behavior, your loved ones will begin to withdraw from you, and feel they must walk on eggshells in your presence.

The reliable man receives greater opportunities. When people see that you can be relied upon, they will give you more challenging tasks and responsibilities that will, in turn, allow you to grow, learn, and become a leader. A boss promotes the reliable employee to higher positions; the professor offers research opportunities to the reliable student; the team picks the reliable man as its captain.

On the other hand, the flakier a man is, the lower people's expectations become of him, and this easily becomes a self-perpetuating cycle, destining him to stay a follower, a bit player in every sphere in which he half-heartedly participates.

The reliable man is given more freedom. The unreliable young man must always be watched; he's kept on a short leash. His boss has to constantly look over his shoulder to make sure he's doing his job and hasn't made another mistake. His parents check in on him even after he's left home to offer reminders to take care of his car, thank his grandma for the birthday money, and make an appointment with the dentist.

The reliable young man receives much less supervision and is given greater responsibility over his time. His boss, his parents, and everyone else knows that if he is simply given the roughest outline of what needs to be done, he'll find a way to do it – and do it well — in his own way.

The reliable man gains a reputation for integrity. The word integrity is related to the roots of words like "integrate" and "entire." In Spanish it is rendered "integro," meaning whole. Integrity thus implies the state of being complete, undivided, intact, and unbroken. Such a state contrasts with one that is scattered, fragmented, and incomplete. When a man has a reputation for integrity, others do not wonder what fragment of him they will get that day, and which fragment they'll be dealing with the next. They know he is a rock of strength on which they can rely.

The reliable man lives with confidence and a clear conscience. In always doing his duty, keeping his promises, and fulfilling his obligations, the reliable man is free from the pangs of regret that haunt less dependable men. Not only can other people count on the reliable man, he knows he can count on himself. This breeds the courage and confidence he needs to take on greater challenges and adventures.

The reliable man leads a simpler life. When you're the same man each day in every situation, when you don't have to think up excuses for breaking your promises, when you don't have to live with the regret of letting others down, you can enjoy a type of simplicity that goes way beyond de-cluttering your closet.

15 Maxims for Being a Reliable Man

"A disregard of promises, finally, is like a fungus, which imperceptibly spreads over the whole character, until the moral perceptions are perverted, and the man actually comes to believe he does no wrong, even in breaking faith with his warmest friends."

–William Makepeace Thayer,
Ethics of Success, 1893

1. Keep your promises. Being a man of your word: this is the cornerstone of reliability. If you tell someone you're going to do something, and do it in X amount of time, you better move heaven and earth to fulfill that promise. This is often easier said than done because of the so-called "Yes…damn" effect: when looking ahead to when a promise will need to be fulfilled, we predict we'll have more time in our schedule, and say yes….but when the day of reckoning finally arrives — damn! — you're just as busy as you always were.

But even when you don't feel like doing something, even when more desirable opportunities arise, you still have to make good on your word. Which is why you should make such grudgingly fulfilled commitments extremely rare by not overextending yourself, which brings us to our next point.

"Never affect to be other than you are—either richer or wiser. Never be ashamed to say, 'I do not know.' Men will then believe you when you say, 'I do know.'

Never be ashamed to say, whether as applied to time or money, 'I cannot afford it.'—'I cannot afford to waste an hour in the idleness to which you invite me—I cannot afford the guinea you ask me to throw away.'

Learn to say 'No' with decision, 'Yes' with caution; 'No' with decision whenever it resists a temptation; 'Yes' with caution whenever it implies a promise. A promise once given is a bond inviolable.

A man is already of consequence in the world when it is known that we can implicitly rely upon him. I have frequently seen in life a person preferred to a long list of applicants for some important charge, which lifts him at once into station and fortune, merely because he has this reputation—that when he says he knows a thing, he knows it, and when he says he will do a thing, he does it."

— Lord Bulwer Lytton, from the Inaugural Address of the Lord Rector of the University of Glasgow, 1856

2. Don't overpromise. The promise of the reliable man is an enormously valuable thing, since it will unswervingly be fulfilled. For this reason, you will find yourself being asked by others to take on more responsibilities and will be offered more opportunities than the flake. Some of these will grant to you valuable chances for growth, learning, and leadership. But some will simply overextend you and take you further away from, not closer to, your goals and priorities.

Thus, being reliable does not mean saying yes to everyone — quite the opposite. The reliable man must use great discretion when making promises to others. The "yes…damn" effect has two main causes, 1) an overly rosy forecast of how busy we'll be at a future date, and 2) the desire to please others. To counteract these causes, you should:

- **Ask yourself whether you could do it tomorrow.** If you feel like there's no way you could do something tomorrow because you're too busy, and you wouldn't rearrange your schedule to make room for it, then you can bet that you won't feel any differently a month from now, and will come to regret making the commitment.
- **Double your estimate for how long you think it will take.** Part of our overly optimistic forecast for the future

is thinking an event or task will take less time than it actually will. When weighing whether to commit to something, double your knee-jerk estimate of how much time it will require of you, to make sure it will really fit in your schedule. Better to over-deliver than overpromise.

- **Give yourself a day to think it over.** It can be hard to say no in the moment — you'll feel pressure to please the asker. So just tell them that you need to look over your schedule, and that you'll get back to them the next day. This will give you time to really think it over instead of answering on impulse and regretting it later. If you decide to decline, it also usually gives you a chance to make the "no" less personal, by simply shooting them an email the following day.
- **Learn how to say "no" firmly but politely.** This is one of the most important skills a young man can master. Don't hedge your no with some "I'll have to sees" and "maybes" — be direct and clear. We often feel like turning others down isn't "nice," but it's much more impolite to commit to something, and then bow out later at the last minute, or to come, but to fulfill the commitment in a half-assed manner.

3. Manage expectations. When you make a promise or take on a job, be careful to be realistic about when and what you will deliver. If you're a salesman or a freelancer, you understandably want to make the thing you're offering seem enticing to attract customers and clients. But inflated expectations can lead to big-time disappointment — sinking your chances of repeat business with the current client and damaging your reputation for potential future ones.

4. Don't leave other people hanging. If you do make a promise that truly dire and unforeseen circumstances prevent you from fulfilling, let the person know as soon as possible. Bite the bullet and don't wait until the last minute to tell them you can't make it. If you're running late, call ahead to let the person you're meeting know instead of letting them wonder where you are.

Always strive to be prompt in your responses to online communication as well. Try your best to reply within 24-48 hours of receiving a text or email, even if just to say, "I can't give you an answer right now, but will look into it, and get back to you as soon as I can," or "Got it. Will get to work!"

"You are now a man, and I am persuaded that you must hold an inferior station in life, unless you resolve, that, whatever you do, you will do well. Make up your mind that it is better to accomplish perfectly a very small amount of work, than to half do ten times as much. What you do know, know thoroughly."

— Sir Fowell Buxton, from a letter to his son

5. Whatever you do, do it well. The maxim: "If something is worth doing, it's worth doing well," has been around for a couple of centuries, and is just as true today as it ever was. Do your best work whether the task is fulfilling and important, or menial and mindless. Some young men feel that it's alright to half-ass work when it's a task that's "beneath" them, saying that they'd put in a real effort if the work was commensurate with their talents and abilities. But it's the man who takes pride in his work, whatever it is, who moves ahead; he who cannot be trusted with little things, will never be trusted with big things.

"In great matters men show themselves as they wish to be seen; in small matters, as they are."

—Nicolas Chamfort

6. Be consistent. Consistency is a huge part of reliability. The guy who gets pumped about an exercise program, works out every day, and then after two weeks falls off the wagon for several months; the student who sometimes churns out A+ papers and sometimes doesn't turn them in at all; the friend who hangs out with you every day but disappears when you ask for a favor; the boyfriend who apologizes for his temper and callous behavior and swears he's going to turn over a new leaf... for the tenth time. These men lack consistency, and thus fail to gain the trust of others, or build faith in themselves.

The reliable man develops consistency by setting goals for himself that stretch and challenge him, but are doable day after day.

"I hate a thing done by halves. If it be right, do it boldly; if it be wrong, leave it undone."

–Bernard Gilpin

7. Finish what you start. A boy picks up one toy or craft or game after another, leaving a trail of half-finished projects through his childhood. A man carefully decides what projects he will begin — he does not rush into things in the heat of blind emotional enthusiasm — and then sees them through to the end.

8. Pull your weight and shoulder your own responsibilities. When you're on a team or working on a group project, other people are counting on you. When you don't fulfill your role, you imperil their success, and unfairly increase their burdens. For example, when you call in sick to work, when you really just want to loaf around, you make your fellow employees work much harder or force someone to work on what was supposed to be their scheduled day off.

"There is nothing like a clean record, the reputation of being square, absolutely reliable, to help a young man along. There is nothing comparable to truth as a man builder. Nothing else will do more toward your real advancement than the resolve, in starting out on your career, to make your word stand for something, always to tell the truth, whether it is to your immediate material interest or not. Truth and honesty make an impregnable foundation for a noble character."
— Orison Swett Marden, *Making Life a Masterpiece*, 1916

9. Be honest. If a news site frequently got a story wrong, readers would soon reject it as unreliable. We also offer "news" and opinions to others, and if they contain falsehoods, people will stop looking to us as a source of enlightenment. We can deceive others in very straightforward ways — lying, cheating, stealing — but in more subtle ways as well — in a look or a gesture, in silence, in telling only one part of a story and leaving out another, in passing along gossip, and so on. Anything that leads people to believe something that isn't true is dishonest.

Another part of being honest is always saying what you mean. Don't tell an acquaintance that you'd love to hang out and you'll give him a call every time you run into him, if you have no intention of following-through. Don't tell a girl you want to stay friends when you break up with her, if you'd really rather go your separate ways altogether.

10. Pay back money and return things in a timely manner. Whether you borrow $100 or a hammer, return the money or item as soon as you can. Your friend will remember that you owe him, but won't want to ask, which can cause a rift in your relationship.

11. Be punctual. If you tell someone that you will meet them at a certain time, you have essentially made them a promise. And if you say you'll be there at 8:00, and yet arrive at 8:15, you have essentially broken that promise. Being on time shows others that *you are a man of your word*.

12. Be fair and consistent in rewards and punishments. A reliable man makes very clear what requirements must be met to earn a reward, and what kinds of behaviors warrant punishment. When those standards are met or violated, he doles out rewards and punishments without regards to favoritism or his current mood. People know exactly what to expect from him, and this builds the resiliency of those under his leadership.

A man who showers one person with praise, and is stingy with another for the exact same accomplishment, or sometimes punishes punitively and sometimes leniently for the same transgression, breeds apathy and "learned helplessness" — a feeling of "what's the point?" — among those he leads. Being consistent with your rewards and punishments is especially important if you aim to raise resilient children. *Esquire Magazine* called this "parenting like a video game." The rules of a video game are predictable — do this and get docked, do this and move ahead. When your kid does something wrong, you *dispassionately* dole out the agreed upon punishment, and hit the reset button — time to try again. When they do something right, you consistently give the agreed upon reward, and let them level up in your trust of them.

"While, then, the stubborn facts may not be altered, we can... make them serve our ends. He who thus adjusts himself to circumstances makes them his friends that hasten to help at every turn, while he who fails so to do is surrounded by enemies that continually annoy and attack."
   – William C. King, *Portraits and Principles of the World's Great Men and Women*, 1898

13. Don't let circumstances dictate your behavior. Your values, ethics, morals, purpose, and so on should not be contingent on the circumstances in which you find yourself. A man who chooses to be happy can be happy anywhere, while the man who wishes to be morose will find reason for complaint in even the most favorable of situations. The reliable man is the same man no matter what befalls him and makes the most of whatever hand he is dealt.

14. Don't collapse in emergencies. Your reliability will be most tested during a crisis. Plenty of men can be there for others and do a job when the sailing is smooth. But when the crap hits the fan they fold like a lawn chair. Fair weather reliability is no reliability at all. The reliable man practices and prepares for emergencies so he knows just what to do in a crisis. And he cultivates the virtues of courage and hardihood, so that when everyone else is running away from chaos, he digs in his heels and starts running towards it.

15. Show up. It is often said that 95% of life is just showing up. I don't know how accurate that number is for life as a whole, but it's certainly spot on when it comes to reliability. Show up to work on time. Show up to the party you promised to attend. Show up to your friend's play, even if he only has a bit part.

Even when you haven't promised someone that you'll be there, if they need you, show up.

I was recently talking to a friend whose mother had just died. She said how surprised she was to see old friends of hers and of her family — some she hadn't seen in two decades — show up at her mom's funeral. She said she hadn't realized how much their presence would mean to her, and how grateful she would feel to see them there. She had previously wondered how well you should know a person to attend their funeral, but now felt it was always a good idea to show up.

Being reliable means that when a friend needs support, he does not even have to ask you or wonder if you'll show. He can say with certainty, *"He'll come."*

DAY 27

How to Shop
for Groceries

This is the one section we didn't originally have in the outline for this book, but when we saw it listed several times when we asked for recommendations at the start, we decided to include it.

I can definitely see why it was requested. There are many chores that parents have their children participate in while they're growing up, but usually mom and dad retain exclusive control over grocery shopping. Thus, when a young man leaves home, he finds himself blinking under the fluorescent lights of the local supermarket, thousands of products stretched out before him. That first outing he may feel a little giddy as he wheels his very own shopping cart around the store, but that thrill quickly turns to dismay when he finds mid-week that even though he dropped some major coin at the register, he now has nothing to eat.

Below we share some basic tips so that you can cruise the aisles of the supermarket with confidence and get the most bang for your buck.

DECIDING WHERE TO SHOP

Back in the old days you either made your own food or bought what you needed from the single general store in town. Now, we have almost an embarrassment of options when it comes to where to procure our food. It can be hard to sort through all those options, so below we provide their pros/cons along with a little description of each:

Traditional Supermarket (Safeway, Walmart Neighborhood Market, Kroger)

- **Pros**: accepts coupons, plenty of in-store specials, large selection of products, fruits and vegetables out of season, customer loyalty card discounts.
- **Cons**: produce is typically trucked in from various parts of the country/world and is not as fresh, more selection can entice you to buy products you don't need, higher prices than discount stores.

A traditional grocery store offers one-stop convenience – you can pick up bacon, toilet paper, and shampoo in one trip. But you pay for this convenience with higher prices on things that aren't on sale or you don't have a coupon for. But if you shop the advertised in-store specials at straight supermarkets, you can save a fair amount.

Warehouse Store (Sam's Club, Costco)

- **Pros**: discounts on groceries, gas, and a wide range of products from suitcases to televisions.
- **Cons**: requires annual membership fees, less product selection, you may not need such huge quantities of something, don't accept coupons other than their own.

Warehouse stores offer discounts to shoppers by selling products in bulk – big pallets of toilet paper or huge jugs of soy sauce. Whether the hassle of this system and the annual membership fee required are worth it is much debated. That you can save a good deal of money on things is not in dispute.

But to expand on the "cons" listed above, it's important to mention a few caveats:

1. People assume that every item at a warehouse store is the best deal in town, but this isn't always the case. You can often get much better prices by using a coupon or taking advantage of an advertised special at a grocery store, and this is true even for things like shampoo and toilet paper.

2. Because of the wide range of products available outside of things like food and paper goods, you can be tempted to buy things you don't need.

3. When you buy something in bulk, you may not be able to use it all up before it goes bad. This is an especially important consideration for the young bachelor, as he may not have room to store big pallets of stuff, and won't be gobbling up groceries like a family of six.

In general, for a young man just heading out on his own, I don't think a warehouse store membership is beneficial. If you do get one, split it with a friend (you can share a card if you go together), and stick with buying non-perishables.

ETHNIC GROCERY STORES

- **Pros**: unique products and cuts of meat, often cheaper prices on produce/meat/spices, fresher meats and produce.
- **Cons**: narrow selection of goods, "American" products (e.g., Oreos) are more expensive.

It can be fun to check out your local Indian, Asian, or Mexican supermarket to see the things they carry that no other store in town does. When I make carne asada, I like to go to the supermercado to get freshly made tortillas and a selection of Mexican pastries.

You may have heard the urban legend that ethnic grocery stores have lower prices on items like meat and produce because they don't have to follow the same safety standards as other establishments. But this is a misconception. The lower prices are due to the store sourcing the products more directly and cutting out the middleman.

In my experience, ethnic grocery stores aren't generally as clean as traditional ones.

OUTLET GROCERY STORE (LOCAL VARIATIONS)
- **Pros**: big discounts on products.
- **Cons**: less fresh food, ever-changing selection, question-able items.

An outlet grocery store stocks what might be termed "super-market hand-me-downs": dented cans, products that are about to hit or have surpassed their "use by" dates, Christmas-themed cereals in July, stuff a traditional store decided not to carry anymore, and so on. You can get some great deals on these "second-rate" items, but you have to shop carefully. Dented cans and expired meat and dairy can make you sick (continue reading for more information about expiration dates).

For those on the Eastern half of the country, Aldi is a different kind of discount grocery store to check out. While groceries at outlet stores are discounted because they're "second-rate," Aldi cuts prices by mainly offering only a small selection of their own decent quality house brand, only accepting cash, debit, or EBT cards (no credit cards or checks), stocking the few aisles with products still in boxes and pallets, and making you bring your own grocery bags and "rent" a shopping cart for 25 cents (you get your quarter back when you return the cart).

NATURAL/HEALTH/ORGANIC GROCERY STORES (WHOLE FOODS, TRADER JOE'S, LOCAL NATURAL FOOD STORES)

- **Pros**: big selection of fresh/natural/organic groceries + unique products + specialty health items (gluten-free, vegetarian/vegan, vitamins/supplements), cheaper bulk items like grains and spices.
- **Cons**: less selection of products overall, higher prices.

While many traditional supermarkets have begun to carry a selection of natural and organic groceries, natural grocery stores have a much wider array of these items and are reliable sources of things like grass-fed beef and free-range chicken. At the same time, if you're looking for Cheetos or cream of mushroom soup, you're out of luck.

Prices at health grocery stores are higher than traditional grocery stores, but the higher prices do (generally) net you a more natural product. And bulk items, like spices and grains, can be cheaper here.

FARMER'S MARKETS

- **Pros**: very fresh and tasty food, a chance to support local farmers.
- **Cons**: higher prices, may only be held once a week, what

is available changes with the seasons.

Many cities and towns hold weekly farmer's markets where farmers in the area come and sell their produce, meat, and baked goods. It's a fun thing to attend and to take a date to, the goods are fresh and delicious, and it's nice to stick it to big agribusiness by supporting local farmers. The pitfall is that the prices can be pretty steep.

So there you have a rundown of your main grocery shopping options. And with these choices come more choices: many people decide to do their shopping at more than one store. For example, you might budget money to buy your meats and produce at a natural food store, while buying your staples at a discount store. Or you might shop at different traditional supermarkets each week according to which store has the best deals on what you need at that time. These advertised specials can be found online and as inserts in the Sunday newspaper. Some stores like Walmart will match the prices of other stores' advertised specials, and that can save you from running from store to store.

Of course many folks find the convenience of getting everything they need at a one-stop-shop like Walmart outweighs any other factor.

There are other things to consider as well:
- By driving around to more than one store to score a deal, will I negate the savings with the gas I burn?
- Is a store's reputation for how they treat their employees important to me?
- If I shop at a big discount store, will I be tempted to buy

more than I need, negating the savings? I don't think this is considered enough. I've lately been doing most of my grocery shopping at a small natural foods store. Not because I have money to burn, but because I found that I spent about the same amount of money shopping there as when I went to Walmart. When shopping at the latter, I'd always end up making unplanned purchases of junk or packaged food (oh cool, PF Chang's in a bag), while at the natural food store, the selection is a lot smaller, I buy less packaged food, and I find it easier to stick to my list. So while the prices are more expensive, I purchase less overall, and the bill comes out about the same.

TIPS FOR GROCERY SHOPPING LIKE A PRO

Always go with a list. To save time and money, always, always create a shopping list before you head to the store, and stick to it religiously. Studies done by the grocery industry have shown that 60 to 70 percent of purchases at the grocery store are unplanned. That pretty much fits my experience. I remember when I first started shopping for myself, I'd just grab things from displays that looked tasty and interesting. This wasn't good for either my waistline or my wallet.

Here's how to create your shopping list:

1. Begin by planning out your weekly menu and then putting the needed ingredients on your list.

2. After you've written the items for your menu, do a quick check on your staples. How's the milk/egg/bread supply? Do you need more paper towels or tin foil? How

are you doing on TP? If you feel like there's something you need, but you can't think of it, run through your daily routine in your mind to jog your memory (first I brush my teeth, then I floss, then I get in the shower, then I wash my hair – oh shampoo! – that's what I needed.) Add needed items.

3. Now take your rough list, and create a master list that will make your shopping trip more efficient by grouping items together that are together at the store. Here's an example:

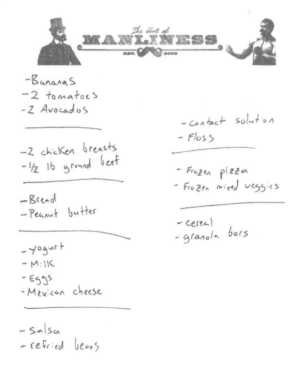

Check the unit price to get the best deal. Instead of simply looking at the overall price when deciding which product to buy, look at the unit price. The unit price tells you the price per pound, ounce, liter, etc. of a product.

Many stores have the unit price right on the shelf label, but it's usually smaller and more discrete than the total price. Here's a picture of Walmart's price labels with the unit price pointed out:

If your store doesn't display the unit price, you can figure it out yourself by simply dividing the price by the number of pounds/ounces/etc. in the package. For example, the unit price for a 10-pound package of flour costing $5.00 is $.50 a pound ($5/10 lbs = $.50).

Breaking a product's price down like this allows you to better compare prices of different items. This is especially important when different brands package the same product in different quantities. In an effort to maximize profits, companies will package and price items in such a way that you'll actually buy the more expensive item on a unit price basis. For example, consumers often intuitively think that if they buy the biggest box on the shelf, they'll get the lowest unit price. For the most part that's true, but not always, so it's worth it to double check.

Some items have what's called a *quantity surcharge*. Grocery stores will often jack up the price on products in large-sized packages, driving the unit price up. Buying the single serving or smaller sized package can actually be the better deal if a larger product has a quantity surcharge. This happens a lot with cereals, so make sure to compare before you decide to buy the big-ol' three-pound box of Cinnamon Toast Crunch.

Go with generic brands when you can. As we discussed in our chapter on being a savvy consumer, generic products can be hit or miss. Many are manufactured in the same factory as the brand name product and simply given a different label. They're discounted because they don't have to spend money on advertising to maintain "brand awareness." Other times, a generic is cheaper because it's not made as well. So just do some experimenting. I always buy the generic first, and only switch if I'm dissatisfied with it.

Skip coupons. Now this is just my opinion. Plenty of people are super into couponing and think it's the bees knees and extremely worthwhile. Personally, I've tried couponing, but the payoff was never worth the time and effort. Most of the coupons you'll find in the Sunday paper are for crap food like Dunk-a-roos and Juicy Juice boxes; it was rarely for stuff I'd buy anyway. We have to remember that coupons aren't printed because food manufacturers want to help out our budget.

Coupons are a marketing strategy to get consumers to purchase something they wouldn't buy in the first place. I've also noticed that coupons get issued for stuff that's already overpriced to begin with. I can save 15 minutes of my time and save the same amount of money buying the generic brand versus clipping a coupon for the name brand. Or I simply choose the brand that the store is running a special on.

Shop on a full stomach. To save money, never shop on an empty stomach. Studies show that when shoppers visit the grocery store hungry, they usually end up spending more money on food. So go shopping after you've eaten a meal, when possible. If your schedule doesn't permit that, at least have a small snack before hitting the supermarket.

Understand the difference between "sell by," "use by," and "best by." It's easy to notice that most food products come with dates stamped on them. But what's the difference between "sell by" and "use by"? I honestly didn't know myself until writing this! But it's a good bit of knowledge to file away as it can help you make purchasing decisions, figure out whether a bargain at a grocery outlet store is a good deal or might make you sick, and prevent you from throwing away perfectly good food (and money).

- **Best by.** Often found on shelf-stable products, the "best by" stamp is not a safety rating, but indicates the point up until which the product will offer the best quality and flavor. After that date, the texture and taste may change, but it can still be safe to consume.

- **Sell by.** Perishables like meat, dairy, and bakery goods are frequently given a "sell by" stamp. This label tells the store how long to display an item on their shelves. You should always buy a "sell by" item before the date given, but it's not a safety indicator, and the product may still be good for days or weeks after you bring it home and the date has expired, as long as you store it properly.
- **Use by.** "Use by" is the only designation that indicates that the product may no longer be safe after that date. It is actually used more often as a "best by" label, but since these products can spoil faster than others, always consume a "use by" product on or before that date to be on the safe side. When buying a "use by" product, make sure you'll have time to consume it before the date given.

When it comes to perishables like milk, always reach to the back of a shelf to grab a carton; the store will put products which are closer to reaching their "sell by" date up at the front of a shelf or on the top of a stack while the fresher ones will be in the back or on the bottom.

Once you bring a product home, cook a "use by" product on or before the date given, and store "sell by" perishables at 40 degrees or below and "best by" items in a cool, dry cabinet.

To figure out how long you can store a "sell by" or "best by" item (or an item without a date), before you have to cook, consume, or freeze it, consult a "keep it or toss it" database like *stilltasty.com*. The answers may surprise you — for example, did you know you can keep eggs for 3-5 weeks after the date on the package? Checking dates can prevent you from throwing away a ton of food! (But always look at the appearance of an item and give it a sniff for spoilage, too, before consuming!)

How to Check If Produce Is Ripe

Picking produce is tricky. You don't want to buy fruits and vegetables that are too ripe (if you buy them and don't eat them right away, they'll go to waste), nor do you want them to be so under-ripe that you'll have to wait a few days before you can eat them.

For the first few years of my adult life, I had no idea how to pick fresh produce. I'd go to the produce section and sort of "ape" what I saw my mom do when I went to the grocery store with her as a boy. I'd pick up fruits and vegetables to squeeze and smell them. The entire time, however, I would be thinking, "I have no clue what I'm doing."

After several trips of me mindlessly fondling the produce, I finally did some research on what I should actually be looking for when selecting it.

Picking Ripe Fruit

- **See it.** For some fruits like apples, bananas, and tomatoes, you can tell it's ripe simply by looking at its color. If you don't plan on using the fruit for a while, it's a good idea to buy it green at the store so it has time to ripen up at home. Avoid fruits with dark spots or bruises, which indicate the fruit has been damaged.
- **Squeeze it.** As fruit ripens, the substances that hold the cells

together break down and convert to water-soluble pectins, which make the fruit become softer and softer. Thus, a soft squeeze is a good test for ripeness. You want the flesh of the fruit to be firm, but give a little bit to the touch. If it's rock hard, it's not ripe; if it's mushy, it's over-ripe. The squeeze test is useful on fruits like peaches, pears, plums, avocados, and kiwis. It's not as helpful on fruits with thick rinds like melons and pineapples. Although if you feel like giving your pineapple a gentle, loving squeeze, that's your prerogative.

- **Smell it.** Chemical changes take place in ripening fruits that produce fruity smells. Sniff the blossom end of the fruit (the end opposite of the stem). You're looking for a light, sweet smell. If it smells sour or overly fruity, it's probably over-ripe.
- **Heft it.** Juiciness is an important attribute for fruits like watermelons, cantaloupe, and tomatoes. To ensure you get the juiciest piece of fruit, pick it up in your hand and heft it. The heavier the fruit, the juicier it's likely to be.

Picking Ripe Vegetables

- **See it.** Look for vegetables that are evenly colored. You want leafy greens that are dark in color. The darker the leaf, the more flavor they have. Some brown spots on lettuce and kale should be expected, but overall they should be nice and green. If a vegetable looks wilted, pass it over.
- **Squeeze it.** Unlike fruit, you want vegetables to be as firm as possible. Vegetables that are wilted and soft just aren't very appetizing. Broccoli, potatoes, carrots, cucumbers, onions, peppers, and cauliflower should all be firm to the touch. Leafy greens like lettuce, kale, and cabbage should snap with a nice crisp sound.

DAY 28

How to
Jump-Start
a Car

355

How to Jump Start a Car

2. Connect one end of the red (*positive*) jumper cable to the positive terminal on the stalled battery.

3. Connect the other red (*positive*) cable clamp to the positive terminal of the good battery.

1. Pull jumper car next to car with dead battery. Make sure both cars are turned off and pop their hoods.

5. Connect the other black (*negative*) cable to a clean, unpainted metal surface under the disabled car's hood. Somewhere on the engine block is a good place. *Do not connect* the negative cable to the negative terminal of the dead battery.

6. Now start the car that's doing the jumping and allow it to run for 2-3 minutes before starting the dead car.

Remove cables in reverse order of how you connected them. Keep the jumped car running for at least 30 minutes to give the battery sufficient time to recharge itself.

4. Connect one end of the black (*negative*) jumper cable to the negative terminal of the good battery.

How to Iron Your Trousers

WRITTEN BY ANTONIO CENTENO

Many young men will likely find themselves dressed in jeans most of the time. But there will be occasions where you'll need to wear a nicer pair of trousers – a job interview, a networking event, a formal church service, and, if you play your cards right, your own graduation! A nicely pressed, non-wrinkled pair of pants finishes off an outfit, and gives you a sharp, put-together look. Having your pants pressed at your local cleaners is one easy option. But for a young man who wants to save a few bucks, or is pressed for time, this is an important skill to know. Learning how to iron your pants yourself will make you more self-sufficient and offer a basic understanding of the clothing you put on.

WHY MEN DO NOT IRON THEIR TROUSERS

1. Fear of damage – Also called "The Shining" (no, not the Stephen King book). Rather, this is what happens when trousers are ironed improperly with too high of a heat setting and the iron is pushed repeatedly across the fabric. The fabric is molded and the weaves are compressed, resulting in a nonporous sheen that makes your trousers look cheap and reduces their lifespan.

2. Lack of information – Google how to iron a dress shirt and you'll find tons of guides and videos out there. How to press trousers? Not so many, and half of them are providing bad advice!

3. They think no one notices – More than half the guys in your office don't iron their trousers or shirts — who is going to notice, right? Wrong — if you have ambition beyond entry-level work, dress for the position you aspire to.

4. They're not even sure they should be ironed – In general, all types of pants should be ironed except cargo pants and jeans (unless you're into the western look). This is because of their informal nature. Wool trousers should be pressed between dry cleanings when needed, such as after unpacking for a business trip. Most cotton trousers, like chinos, are washed at home, and should be pulled from the dryer slightly damp. They should be ironed at this point for the easiest time pressing. Synthetic dress slacks are often dry cleaned, although this isn't really needed, and should be pressed between wearings, when wrinkles appear.

The ironing instructions below will leave a crease down the center of the pant legs. For more casual pants like khakis, you may want to iron the pants without a crease.

WHAT YOU'LL NEED
- Ironing board
- Iron
- Distilled or purified water
- Spray bottle (unnecessary if the iron has a built-in spray nozzle)
- Clean trousers

IMPORTANT POINTS
- Press the iron (pick it up, put it down); do not push it across the clothing.

- Examine the trousers for stains and remove the stains/dirt BEFORE ironing. Otherwise you will have a permanent stain.
- Ironing time is not an exact science — but the rule should be as little time as it takes to press out the wrinkles. Steam helps **a lot**. I start with 2 seconds, then modify the time depending on the fabric thickness and reaction to pressing.
- Ensure the iron is the **correct** temperature for your trousers. For example, wool can easily be damaged by too much heat. You need to let the iron cool and make sure it is set correctly when ironing trousers after doing shirts (which are normally made from cotton and thus need a higher temperature setting). For this reason I always recommend ironing your trousers before ironing your shirts.

SETTING UP THE IRON

You can mostly follow manufacturer's directions for this step, but the basics are simple:
- Fill the water reservoir if there is one.
- Set the heat for the fabric you're ironing — use the iron's guide or check the tag on the trousers for the appropriate heat.
- Turn the iron on and let it heat up before use.

You want a bit of steam when you're pressing trousers, so use a steam iron, and if possible, one with a nozzle that lets you spray water as you go. If your iron doesn't have a nozzle, keep a spray bottle handy to spray the trousers down ahead of the iron.

How to Press Your Trousers

I divided pressing your trousers into three parts with a total of ten steps.

Part I — Set-Up & Top of Your Trousers

Step 1: Double Check Your Temperature and Trouser Cleanliness

Check the trousers for stains or dirt and remove before ironing. Next, check the label, and ensure the iron is set for that type of fabric.

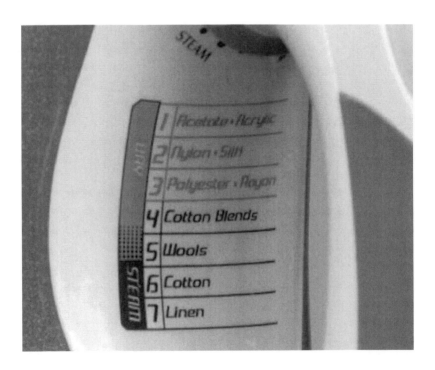

When ironing a blended fabric, choose the lowest (coolest) setting of the two fabrics. If you are ironing a 70% wool/polyester blend, you would start at 3 and maybe go up to a 4. Lower temperatures will take longer to set a crease, but they are less likely to damage your pants.

Step 2: Iron the Linings of the Pockets

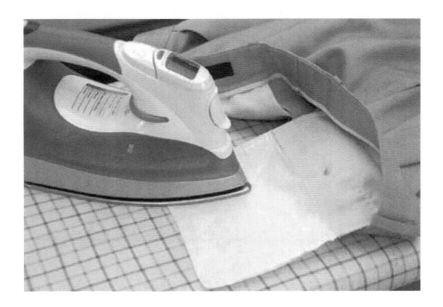

Most dress trousers have inside pocket linings. Although no one will ever see these, if they are severely wrinkled and you wear your trousers close fitted, an impression of the wrinkles might be visible. Prevent this by smoothing out the lining. Note that linings are often made from cotton. You might have to start with a hotter temperature if you are ironing wool trousers, and then let the iron cool for 5 minutes before pressing the rest of the pants.

Step 3: Iron the Waistband and Top Part of the Trouser

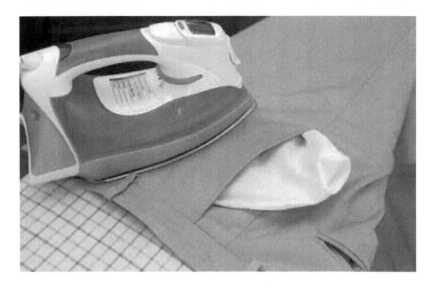

Turn front pockets out and then press the iron on the top of the leg. Lift the iron up, reinsert the pocket, and continue to press along the top of the trouser, paying special attention to pleats and re-forming any folds. Remember, we are pressing and lifting the iron — not pushing it along the fabric.

Move to the seat of the trousers, and pull out the back pockets. Press these areas and then move up to the waistband.

Finally, move to the opposite front side of the pants, turning the pocket inside out and repeating the process.

PART II — PRESSING YOUR TROUSERS' CREASES

Step 4: Mark the Trouser Crease at the Bottom

Lay the trousers flat on the ironing board with the cuffs right at one end, waist draped over the far end. The waist can hang off a bit if the board is short.

Flip a trouser leg up and off the board so that you're working with just one leg, and lay it flat on the board. Look inside the cuff and find the two seams.

Arrange the trouser leg so that one inseam lies right on top of the other, dead center of the flat leg. With the inseams in the center, the edges of the trouser leg are where you want to press the crease.

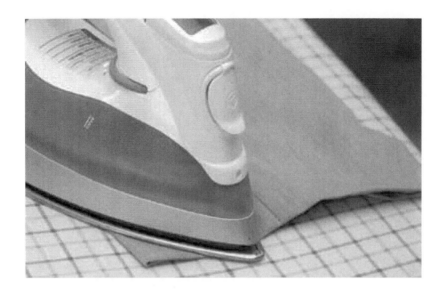

Spray the cuff with a bit of water and press down gently on each side of the trouser leg. This should leave a visible crease at the cuff and an inch or two up the leg.

Step 5: Mark the Crease at the Top

Find the same two vertical inseams and match them up, one on top of the other, just like you did above in Step 4, but this time at the top of the pants.

Lay the top of the trouser leg flat with the inseams centered.

Wet the outer edge of the trouser leg and use the iron to gently press a crease into place along that edge, about six inches down from the waistband.

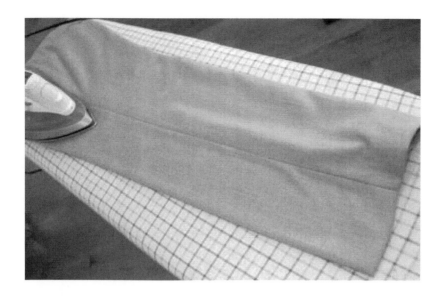

Don't press the crease all the way up to the waistband. The bottom of the pockets (on the inside of the trousers) is a good place to stop, or if you have pleated trousers you can just press the crease right up to the bottom of the side pleats.

Step 6: Press the Front Crease

Now that you've got the start and finish of the crease marked, it's just a matter of connecting the dots. If the inseams are still set one atop the other, the crease should be the very edge of the trouser leg as it lies flat.

Press gently down in one spot with the iron. Then lift the iron, move up a bit, and do it again, **always pressing straight down rather than pushing and sliding along the crease.**

Work all the way up from the marker at the cuff to the marker just below the pockets. It's worth reaching inside the trouser and pulling the pocket aside so that you don't accidentally press its shape into the trouser leg while you're working on the crease.

Step 7: Press the Back Crease

The back crease (the one that follows the inside of your leg) should be directly opposite the front crease, also at the very edge of the trouser leg as it lies flat. Repeat the same process you used to create the front crease, again pressing straight down, gently pressing to set the crease in place, and then lifting the iron back up again.

Step 8: Press Down the Trouser Leg

Once you've got your creases set you can press the center of the trouser leg between the creases to get out any small wrinkles or folds. Use the same motion you've been using: press the iron flat, pick it back up, and repeat again a little further along.

If you're worried about the trouser fabric, you can cover it with a thin, clean white cloth and press through that. In the case of delicate or napped weaves (such as grey flannel trousers) a barrier helps prevent "shine," which is the slicked-down look you get when you've ironed too hard or at too high of a temperature.

You do not need to press both sides of the same trouser leg.

Step 9: Repeat for the Other Trouser Leg

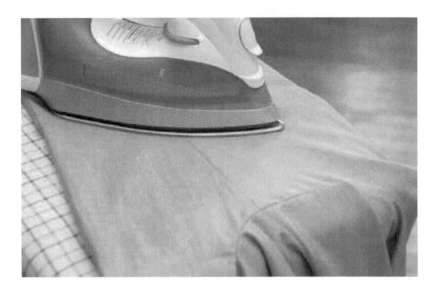

Once you've pressed the creases and the leg, you're ready to switch to the other side. Repeat the process above.

Step 10: Iron Seat and Front of Trousers as Needed

The seat and front of the trousers don't usually need pressing the way the crease does, but if you do want to press them be sure to turn the pockets inside-out before applying the iron. You can actually slip the pants over the ironing board (as if you were putting the pants onto the board instead of your legs) to keep the front and back panels separate, allowing you to iron them one at a time.

Once you're done ironing both legs (and the rest of the trousers, if desired), be sure to hang them to let them dry completely before wearing. If you wear the trousers damp you'll work the crease right back out, wasting all your hard work.

Limitations – The Case for an Occasional Professional Pressing

Trousers should be periodically pressed by a professional. The reason is that professional dry cleaners have a special iron and vacuum board that uses a combination of steam being pressed in and immediately sucked out. This produces impeccably ironed pleats, which can last for a week or more worth of wearings.

DAY 30

How to
Handle Stress

———◆———

375

Whenever we look back on the past, our minds have a tendency to cast things in a warm, rosy glow – our memories invariably focus on the good parts and gloss over the bad. Which is why, when those who are removed a few years from their college days reminisce about that time, all they typically remember are the parties, the girls, the spring breaks, and so on.

What they forget is…the stress.

The stress of both holding down a job and being a student, the stress of stretching a meager budget each month, the stress of breaking up with someone you thought you'd spend your life with, the stress of fighting with a roommate who was once your best friend and is now your sworn enemy, and of course, the stress of cranking out a 20-page research paper and struggling to remember chemistry formulas on your final exams.

Make no mistake about it: the life of a young man is often quite glorious and free, but there will also be times when you feel utterly overwhelmed. Sure, a lot of adults tend to scoff at a young man's stress — "You think you're busy now? Wait until you have a wife, three kids, and a full-time job!" And these men are right, in a way – your total amount of stress will tend to increase as you age and take on more responsibilities, and you'll probably look back on college and think, "What the heck was I so worried about?" But it's all relative, isn't it? The stress of a young man is both unique (I wouldn't trade the pressure of a real job for being tested on my ability to regurgitate information again) and new – you haven't yet accumulated the life experiences that will help you see that what feels like the end of the world now, is just another bump in the road.

All of which is to say, the stress you will experience after leaving home is real, and learning how to deal with it is one of the most important skills a young man can master. Since it is true that your stress will likely increase with age, learning how to manage it now will prepare you to live happily and confidently not just into your 20s, but for the rest of your life as well.

With that truth in mind, today we take you through a comprehensive primer designed to help you understand what stress is, how it can negatively affect both body and mind, and how you can easily and effectively manage it.

WHAT IS STRESS?

Stress is your body's reaction to circumstances in which it feels it needs more strength, stamina, and alertness in order to survive and thrive. Any perceived challenge or threat to your well-being can induce a stress response. This response signals your nervous system to release the hormones adrenaline, noradrenaline, and cortisol into your bloodstream, which gets you revved up and ready for action: your heart rate, blood pressure, sweating, and breathing increase, your blood vessels dilate to speed blood flow to your muscles, your pupils dilate to enhance your vision, and your liver releases stored glucose for your body to use as energy. In primitive times, this so-called "fight or flight" response instantly primed your body to deal with danger.

Thus, while many people view stress as an exclusively bad thing, it can in fact be either positive or negative. In the face of an immediate challenge — a job interview, a big presentation, a difficult test — the stress response puts you on your toes and can improve your performance and ability to handle the pressure. It also lends excitement to life; when you feel nervous butterflies before asking a girl out, or getting on a roller coaster, that's stress too. It might seem like a 100% stress-free life would be incredible, but after a while, a state of perpetual calm would begin to feel flat, stale, and boring (at least for those of us who have not achieved total zen!).

Stress only becomes a problem in the face of two main factors. The first is stress overload. The amount of stress you feel given a certain set of circumstances is directly proportional to the degree in which you feel your skills and resources (including time) are adequate in addressing them. This state of competence can be based on either reality or one's own optimistically or pessimistically rendered self-assessment. A man who enjoys and is talented at public speaking will feel much less stress before making a presentation than a man who is shy and speaks awkwardly; a man who completes an assignment over the course of a week will feel much less stressed than the man who waits to work on it until the night before; a man who is much less confident in dating women and what he has to offer them will feel much more devastated when a girl dumps him than a man who has little doubt he'll soon meet someone else. Instead of getting us revved up for action, stress that seems too big to handle can feel crushing, leaving us feeling overwhelmed and too paralyzed to do anything at all.

The second instance stress becomes a problem is when the set of circumstances causing it becomes chronic. The stress response was originally designed to help humans deal with *immediate* threats and challenges – after the adrenaline rush, our nervous systems quickly returned to stand-by mode in preparation for the next challenge. *Saber-toothed tiger! Throw spear! Tiger dead! Whoo, relax time. Me go back to making cave paintings.* But in modern times, our stressors can go on and on and on. As much as we might like to, we can't spear our annoying roommate or co-worker. Instead, we have to put up with him day after day. And day after day, this chronic stress causes our bodies to dump out low levels of stress hormones. Unfortunately, a steady of dose of something that was supposed to be rare and fleeting can make us physically and emotionally sick.

THE DAMAGING EFFECTS OF TOO MUCH STRESS

Too much stress can do a number on both your body and mind, causing everything from diarrhea and constipation, to tension headaches and hair loss. Below we describe more of the deleterious effects of stress:

Weight gain. At the height of your stress response, you will likely experience a decreased appetite. But once the stress starts to wane, the cortisol that was released into your bloodstream may spur you to eat sugary, carbohydrate-rich foods. This made sense back in primitive times: the fight or flight response usually preceded a bout of physical exertion (get that mammoth!), and after the stress had passed, it was time to replenish your body. These days, when you may experience the stress response while remaining chained to your desk, gobbling down donuts as you descend from your stress peak will only lead to a primordial-sized gut.

Decreased libido and erectile dysfunction. Cortisol also decreases testosterone production, which in turn can depress a man's libido and cause erectile dysfunction. If you want to enjoy a healthy sex drive in adulthood, you'll need to get a handle on your stress today.

Increased blood pressure. Cortisol, along with the other hormones that are released when we're stressed, causes our hearts to beat faster and constrict our blood vessels in order to prime our bodies for fight or flight. Fine in the short term, but prolonged stress can lead to hypertension, and all its attending health problems.

Insomnia. With cortisol still pumping through your veins, even after the height of a stressful experience has passed, you may find yourself still too revved up to sleep. This inability to get some shut-eye is often compounded by other factors that frequently attend stressful times — caffeine consumption, and racing, worried thoughts.

Hyper-emotionality. When you're stressed and your willpower is depleted, you become more emotional. Hyper-emotionality doesn't necessarily mean that you'll become a blubbering mess at a drop of the hat, though that is a common response of individuals who are over-stressed. Rather it means that all your emotions — sadness, anger, even happiness — are in overdrive. With the rational part of your brain no longer in control, you're more susceptible to outbursts of all kinds.

Social isolation. A common response to stress is to retreat to our "bunker" and isolate ourselves from other people. As we'll discuss further down, while it's certainly okay to get some alone time when you're feeling stressed, too much isolation can actually contribute to your anxiety.

Poor concentration and memory. While some stress can make us more mentally nimble, chronic stress depletes our willpower and turns us into dolts. Studies show that individuals who experience stress over a long period of time demonstrate poorer concentration, decreased memory, and a reduced decision making capacity.

Fatigue. According to the American Psychological Association, 25% of men report experiencing physical and mental fatigue several times a week. Stress is one of the biggest contributors to that tuckered out condition. Physical tension and mental worry, along with a diminishment in testosterone, drains our bodies and makes us feel sluggish and tired.

Weakened immune system. You may have heard that all stress is bad for your immune system, but recent studies have shown that short bursts of stress can actually boost it. When your mind senses a coming crisis, stress hormones muster immune cells to potential "battlefields" in the body — tissues, organs, and mucous membranes that are particularly sensitive to infection. In primitive times, the fight of flight response was typically triggered in situations like hunting or combat where physical wounds were a likely outcome, and these immunity "soldiers" stood at the ready to stave off infection and heal these wounds as soon as they formed. But, once again, a response that was beneficial a thousand years ago has been hijacked by the ongoing stress of modern life. The constant drilling of your immunity troops in preparation for a non-existent emergency eventually wearies and weakens them, leaving you vulnerable to infections and inflammation.

Depression. Chronic stress reduces neurotransmitters in the brain like serotonin and dopamine, which help regulate things like appetite, energy, and sleep, in addition to balancing our moods and contributing to our sense of well-being. A diminishment of these neurotransmitters can cause depression directly, but can lead to it indirectly as well by creating a circular pattern of negative behavior. You have trouble sleeping, so you don't feel like exercising in the morning, which makes you feel more stressed out, so you eat more, which makes you feel more sluggish, which makes you not want to go out and socialize…and on the circle spirals, potentially into depression.

Increased alcohol consumption, smoking, and drug use. Men tend to deal with stress by looking for an escape from it. Oftentimes, that escape is alcohol, smoking, and drugs. While many a well-balanced man won't experience any ill-effects from a nightcap to take the edge off a stressful day, it becomes a problem when one glass turns to four. Heavy alcohol or drug use can lead to a whole host of relationship and health problems, and does nothing to mitigate the source of the stress — it may actually exacerbate it.

HOW TO MANAGE STRESS EFFECTIVELY

Reading over all those stress-induced maladies may have left you feeling stressed about being stressed! But don't worry: most stress is very manageable as long as you commit to doing the small, daily maintenance tasks that will keep your stress from reaching the point where it begins to feel crushing.

As we mentioned above in the "What is Stress?" section, negative stress is generally the result of two factors: 1) Not feeling like our skills, talents, and resources (including time) are adequate to handle a threat or challenge, and 2) chronic stress-producing circumstances that last for days, weeks, even years.

Thus, when it comes to managing stress, you need to take a double-pronged approach that includes preventing these factors from occurring in the first place, and learning how to mitigate them when prevention is impossible.

Develop your resiliency. A huge part of dealing with stress has nothing to do with the actual stressor, but how you handle that stressor. A situation one man navigates with confident ease can cause another man to completely fall apart. Thus, the foundational block in your ability to manage stress is developing the trait of resiliency. Being resilient encompasses the way in which you both act and react in the world — your ability to both quickly bounce back from challenges and trials and to face the world head-on with courage and confidence. Without a resilient attitude and approach to life, all of the stress-reducing methods below amount to rearranging the deck chairs on the Titanic.

The path to developing resilience cannot be explained in just a few sentences. Luckily, a couple of years ago, we wrote a comprehensive, 7-part series on the subject. It includes both a conceptual framework to help you understand the nature of resilience as well as practical methods to develop the trait. I really believe it's a must-read for a man of any age. You can find the series at: *www.artofmanliness.com/tag/resiliency.*

Exercise. *If you take only one stress-reducing strategy from this list, let it be this: make exercise a regular habit.* Researchers have found that exercise is just as effective as antidepressants in treating clinical depression and increases the levels of endocannabinoid molecules in our blood, the same endocannabinoids that are responsible for the calming pleasure produced by the consumption of marijuana.

Exercise not only treats stress, it may also help prevent it as well; preliminary studies are beginning to show that the small amount of physical and mental stress you experience when you exercise acts sort of like an inoculation to high-stress events later, creating brain cells that are better able to deal with anxiety, or in other words, a more stress-resistant brain. To make your exercise doubly-effective, do your workout outside, for the reasons we'll explain next.

Get out in nature. In nature, body and mind get a chance to rejuvenate. In a study done in Japan, researchers found that after a 20-minute walk in the forest, participants had "lower concentrations of cortisol, lower pulse rate, lower blood pressure, greater parasympathetic nerve activity, and lower sympathetic nerve activity" than subjects who spent time in the city. In layman's terms? Walking in the woods mellows you out. In a follow-up study, time spent in nature increased feelings of vigor and decreased the feelings of anger, anxiety, and depression.

So instead of spending every Saturday sacked out on the couch watching football, start making time for regular hikes in the woods. Your inner-Thoreau will thank you.

Meditate. Numerous studies have shown that simple mindfulness meditation can reduce and even eliminate many of the negative physiological and psychological symptoms of chronic stress. While you're meditating, blood pressure normalizes, breathing and heart rate slows, and your adrenal glands produce less cortisol. Participants in meditation studies often report lower anxiety, worry, and tension levels. Moreover, regular meditation actually rewires your brain and makes you more resilient in the face of stress.

The beauty of meditation is that you don't even have to meditate that long to get the benefits. Just 20 minutes a day will do the trick, and you'll start noticing the benefits in just a few weeks.

Make a list of what's stressing you out. Sometimes when we have a bunch of things that are worrying us and a long list of things to do, all of these stressors swirl together in a big cloud of restlessness and agitation. We feel overwhelmed, but the cloud makes it hard for us to even articulate exactly why. When this happens, take some time to make a list of everything you're worried about. Offloading them from your brain to paper will help your cranium to relax. This is, in fact, one of the things Dwight D. Eisenhower did to relieve his stress when the burden of deciding when to launch D-Day grew crushingly heavy.

Now, make an action/to-do list by looking at each item on your worry list. Write down small, specific, immediate things you can do to take care of each stressor.

Get plenty of sleep. Sleep and stress create somewhat of a catch-22 problem. Our bodies and minds need sleep to help manage and cope with stress, but stress can oftentimes prevent us from getting the sleep we need! While we could devote an entire chapter to how to improve your slumber, here are a few quick things you can do to get the best night's sleep possible, even when you're feeling tense:

- Meditate twenty minutes before hitting the sack to calm and relax your mind and body.
- Write down all your worries before getting into bed so you're not thinking about them while you're trying to get to sleep. As we just mentioned, this is an effective stress-reducing tactic anytime, but it's particularly effective right before bed.
- Turn off the computer and TV an hour before going to bed. The light from electronic screens suppresses the body's natural melatonin production, a hormone which helps lull you into sleep.
- Speaking of melatonin, consider taking a melatonin supplement right before going to bed. It can help you relax and

get to sleep quicker (and based on my experience, have crazy dreams).

- Make sure your room is nice and cool. Studies show the optimal temperature for sleep is somewhere between 60 to 68 degrees (brrrr!). If you don't want to run the A/C that low all night, get a fan, keep your sleepwear light (or nonexistent), and don't use heavy blankets or comforters.
- Play some white noise. White noise blocks distracting sounds as well as provides a relaxing sound that will soothe you into sleep. This can particularly help if you have night owl roommates who stay up and make noise after you've turned in, or if you live in the heart of a noisy city. A desktop fan is a great white noise source. Or you can download white noise soundtracks to play while you're sleeping. I used a free white noise generator (*www.simplynoise.com*) while in law school for my power naps, speaking of which…

Take a nap. The simple nap is a powerful thing that offers a whole host of amazing benefits, including increased alertness, a boost in your learning and working memory, and greater creativity. It's also a potent stress-fighter: napping releases growth hormones and serotonin, which balances your cortisol, soothes your stabbiness, and leaves you feeling content and rejuvenated.

Reduce caffeine consumption. Caffeine increases cortisol and adrenaline production in your body, which may make you feel better in the short-term, but will increase your jagged, stressed-out feeling in the long-term. Cut back on caffeine and try to avoid it after 2pm to ensure you get a good night's sleep.

Stick to a routine. The more out of control you feel, the more stressed out you'll be. While we can't control everything that happens to us during the day, by taking charge of the things we *can* control, we can greatly reduce our anxiety. One way to feel more in control of your life is by establishing and sticking to routines: exercise routines, morning and evening routines, work routines. Anything you do frequently, try to make it routine. The more your mind knows what to expect next, the more calm and confident it will feel.

Plan your week. Much of the stress I experienced in college was created because I didn't manage my time well. I'd forget due dates, wait until the last minute to write a paper, and schedule appointments that conflicted with other obligations. When I started planning my week, things markedly improved. Having a weekly plan will ensure you don't forget important stuff or overextend your commitments like I did. Moreover, having a plan makes you feel in control, which as we just discussed, keeps stress at bay.

Get social. As I mentioned above, a common response to stress (especially for us men) is to become a hermit. I'm that way. Sometimes I just need to be alone so I can sort through stuff. While it's perfectly fine and healthy to get some alone time when you're stressed, if you're still feeling frazzled after some solitude, call up a buddy or two to hang out. Studies show that social interaction does wonders for reducing stress. Our bodies release anti-stress, feel-good hormones like oxytocin when we're around people who care for us. Plus, friends and family can offer some much needed advice and perspective that can help you manage and sort through whatever's burdening you; while you should strive to be self-reliant as much as possible, there's no shame in calling up mom and dad when you've reached the end of your rope.

One bird at a time. I read a book a few years ago about writing by Anne Lamont that had some advice that I think is applicable to managing stress effectively. From the book *Bird by Bird*:

> "Thirty years ago my older brother, who was ten years old at the time, was trying to get a report on birds written that he'd had three months to write. [It] was due the next day. We were out at our family cabin in Bolinas, and he was at the kitchen table close to tears, surrounded by binder paper and pencils and unopened books on birds, immobilized by the hugeness of the task ahead. Then my father sat down beside him, put his arm around my brother's shoulder, and said. 'Bird by bird, buddy. Just take it bird by bird.'"

When you're feeling overwhelmed and stressed by the things that are piling up, just take them "one bird at a time." Instead of focusing on the enormity of everything you have to do, break things up into their component parts and do one thing at a time until you're done. Concentrate on simply putting one foot in front of the other.

It will get done and over with. Something that helps me when I'm stressed out to the point where it feels like the world is going to end, is simply to tell myself, "It will get done and will be over with." Maybe you'll have to stay up all night to finish it, maybe what you turn in won't be as good as it could have been, but regardless of what happens, that due date or scheduled meeting will come and go, you'll accept the consequences, and life will move on. You can look at the clock, and think, "Okay, at 3:00pm tomorrow, this will be resolved one way or another." For whatever reason, thinking this helps me settle down and get going on whatever I can do.

Start saying "NO." A big source of stress in my life has been over-committing myself. I'd say "yes" to just about anything because, 1) I'm sort of a people pleaser, and 2) I didn't want to miss out on any opportunity that might further my goals. After enduring the stress of managing an overbooked schedule one time too many, I've had to learn to say no. Don't be like me. Don't "should" on yourself, and learn how to say "no" early on in your adult life.

IF YOU'RE FEELING OVERWHELMED, GET HELP

If you're still feeling overwhelmed after doing all that you can to manage your stress on your own, seek professional help immediately from a school counselor or therapist. Reaching out for help, especially for emotional or psychological problems, is hard for men to do. It requires us to talk about emotions and be vulnerable. Plus, we often view getting help as a sign of weakness.

If you feel like you're headed off to the deep end because of stress, don't let the fear of looking "unmanly" keep you from getting the help you need. Men experiencing depression or chronic stress are much more likely than women to abuse alcohol, resort to violence, or attempt suicide. A trained counselor or therapist can walk you through ways to cope with your stress that don't involve harming yourself or others.

If you're at college, go visit the student support center. They should have trained counselors that you can talk to confidentially, for free.

If you're not in college, but can't afford a therapist, try these affordable options as suggested by Everyday Health:

- **Community mental health centers.** Most states and cities have agencies that provide mental health services with trained therapists at a reduced rate. To find a community health center near you, simply Google the name of your city + "community mental health center."

- **Non-profit mental health organizations.** Two non-profit groups – National Alliance of Mental Illness and Mental Health America – have chapters throughout the country that provide affordable individual and group therapy. Visit their respective websites and find a chapter near you.

- **College psychology and therapy departments.** Visit your local college campus to see if they provide discounted mental health services to the public. Many psychology and therapy departments have clinics staffed by graduate students that work with patients under the close supervision of faculty members.

- **Group therapy.** Group therapy is usually much more affordable than one-on-one therapy. Do a Google search to find group therapy sessions near you that focus on stress and anxiety issues.

DAY 31

A Place
for Everything
and Everything
in its Place

•◦•

A s this book draws to a close, we'd like to use the final section to discuss a saying your grandfather was probably quite fond of:

"A place for everything and everything in its place."

Your great-grandfather likely used that maxim too, and his grandfather as well. It actually first appeared in print way back in 1640. The saying was born among sailors, who needed to both keep things orderly in the tiny galleys and cabins below deck, and to make sure all their tools and ropes were placed and secured properly up above, so that things didn't wash overboard when the ship was rocked by storms and waves.

"First then, while you are little boys, let there be order in everything. Try and have a place for everything and everything in its place. If your father has things in that way, see that you place everything back after using it. Hours, days, yea, months and years, are wasted by too many in hunting tools and farming implements; time thus wasted is time needlessly lost, precious time that will never return...I mention this first because it is first in importance. It governs your every act through life. If you start life thus and have a place for everything, you cannot fail to make good farmers."
- Report of the Secretary of the Iowa State Agricultural Society, 1865

"A place for everything and everything in its place" came ashore in the 19th century, and was adopted most rigorously by farmers, who owned and used a wide variety of tools and pieces of equipment, and who couldn't afford to leave them to rust in the rain or exposed to elements during winter. Keeping track of their tools ensured they could get to work when they needed to, and there was always plenty of work to be done.

The maxim was subsequently taken up by men in all trades and businesses, white and blue collar alike, who saw how having a set place for their tools and papers, both at home and at work, contributed to their success. The standard espoused in old books was for a man to be able to dress himself in the dark or find any tool in his shed with his eyes closed.

While a man's tools and necessities may have changed over the centuries, the wisdom in "a place for everything and everything in its place" remains the same. Whether at school, work, or home, creating a system of order for your possessions will create numerous benefits in your life.

THE IMPORTANCE OF HAVING A PLACE FOR EVERYTHING AND EVERYTHING IN ITS PLACE

"Soldiers of every grade must especially avoid slovenliness: they must bear in mind the proverb, 'A Place For EVERYTHING AND EVERYTHING IN ITS PLACE'...When a soldier can bring himself to be habitually exact in small things, he may be safely regarded as reliable in important matters: but he who is negligent over apparent trifles, will find it difficult, if not impossible, to be punctual on occasions of the greatest moment."

- The Manual of the Patriotic Volunteer on Active Service in Regular and Irregular War, 1855

Having a place for everything and everything in its place saves time (and sometimes opportunities, too). Do you know someone (perhaps yourself!) who spends ten minutes looking for his keys every single morning? Or a gent who every time he leaves the house, must turn it inside-out searching for his wallet? When you have a set place for all of your possessions, you can grab them and go. You'll never be late for a job interview, date, or other important event for a silly reason like not being able to find something you need.

If you're in the habit of haphazardly dropping things around the house, you may do so because you feel it takes too much time to put them in their proper places, or because you're just too tired from a long day of work. But by spending and expending a minute of time and a bit of energy now, you'll save yourself from a ten-minute hunt and a lot of hassle the next day.

Having a place for everything and everything in its place saves money. Sometimes a hunt for a lost item comes up empty – it is never found again, forcing you to buy a replacement. You don't have any idea what happened to it – and that's precisely the problem. There's no set place you keep it, so it could have ended up anywhere.

Sometimes a misplaced item is eventually found – but because it was stored carelessly, it was damaged, and you still have to buy another.

In the chapter about being a savvy consumer, we mentioned that a man should not seek to own a great many things, but that those things he does possess should be of good quality. Well, once a man obtains a quality item, he must then take care of it in order to make it last. To live the principle of "a place for everything and everything in its place," is to refuse to follow the dictums of a disposable society.

Having a place for everything and everything in its place will make life smoother and less stressful. As we've mentioned a few times during this series, keeping your place in order gives you a sense of peace and confidence, and conserves your willpower. Being able to get out the door without first running around like a headless chicken only adds to this invaluable sense of calm and control.

Having a place for everything and everything in its place prepares you for an emergency. At boot camp, members of the armed forces are rigorously drilled in strict discipline — their uniforms, beds, and lockers must all be kept just so. For a soldier, attention to little details can mean the difference between life and death. He needs to know where his equipment is every moment — an attack can come any time so he must be always ready to spring into action.

While your abode may never come in for a shelling, it's nice to know that if you ever had to run out the door quickly or jump out of bed in the middle of the night, you could dress yourself, grab what you needed, and be gone in a flash. By the way, according to ITS Tactical, the proper order of dressing when awakened during such a crisis is pants, socks, then shoes.

A Place for Everything

Now obviously, in order to have everything in its place, you have to establish the places you're going to put your things. Your selection of places shouldn't be done willy-nilly, either; if they're inconvenient or ill-chosen, you won't use them, and the habit of putting things there won't stick. The place should be intuitive — putting your stuff in it should require the least possible thought and effort. It should be entirely natural. You're not going to want to climb on a chair to reach a shelf to retrieve and replace something every day, for example. The place you choose to put something has to preserve the quality of the item and protect it from damage as well.

Of course there are as many methods for storing things as there are different items to be stored, and every man will have his own system. Below I walk you through the possible placement of some of the most common possessions for men, as well as offer my personal suggestions on how to organize and store them.

Pocket Contents

We men often carry around a lot in our pockets — smartphone, wallet, pocketknife, handkerchief, keys — and so on. We need these items every day, so they should be as easy as possible to grab each morning when we head out the door.

Key hook. The minute you step through the door — keys go up on the key hook. Now this isn't strictly necessary if you have a dresser valet/box (see below) into which you plan to deposit your keys along with the rest of the contents of your pockets when you change into your lounging wear or pajamas. But even then, if you share the car with someone else or don't have a habit of putting your keys back into your pocket and instead tend to plop them on the counter or couch, the key hook still comes in handy. There will also be times when you want to retrieve something from your car, but don't want to walk into your bedroom to get the keys.

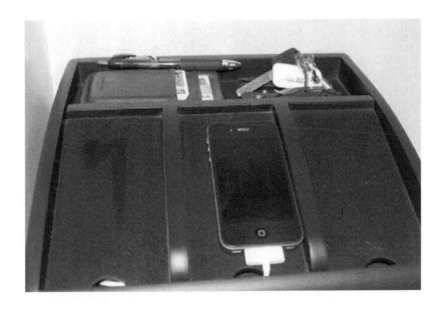

Put your phone, pocketknife, wallet, spare keys, etc. into a dresser valet or other receptacle.

Dresser valet. Instead of dumping all of your pocket accoutrements on top of your dresser at the end of the day, depositing various items around the house, or leaving them in the pockets of the pants sitting in your hamper, place them all in a dresser valet. That way in the morning you can grab everything you need without spending ten minutes looking for your phone and keys.

Nice dresser valets with drawers and chargers for your phone and whatnot are available, but if you're just starting out and on a budget, a $3 basket from Hobby Lobby or even a topless shoebox will do — anything that keeps your stuff together in one place will work fine and dandy.

Kate got me this coin bank for Christmas one year. It's made with the door of an old post office box.

Coin bank. Coins always somehow end up in every conceivable nook and cranny in your house. So every man should have a bank in which to place his change. It's really worthwhile to pick change up wherever you see it at home and when you're out and about as well, and then to deposit it in your bank at the end of the day. I knew a guy who would actually throw away his pennies! Foolishness! Just save your coins for a long time, and then put them into rolls, and exchange the rolls for cash at the bank (unless they have a handy coin-counting machine you can dump your whole loose stockpile into) — you'll be surprised how much green stuff your pocket change will amount to. There's something so satisfying about turning your coins into cash.

I have a wallet that also holds my iPhone. I find that keeping them together this way is quite handy.

Wallet. If you don't keep your wallet organized, it can quickly swell to George Costanza-sized proportions. An overstuffed wallet looks silly when you pull it out, is uncomfortable to carry in your pants, and makes your jacket lopsided when kept in a jacket pocket (not to mention possible back problems if you're sitting on it all day). A giant wallet can also create creases in your pants or jacket which can shorten the life of the garment.

So clean out your wallet regularly, and only put things in it that belong there:

- Keep: Cash, credit cards, ID cards, business cards, photos of loved ones
- Remove: Discount club membership and library cards (keep in car, or grab for a specific trip when you'll need them),

Social Security card (very risky if wallet is stolen — keep at home), condoms (can degrade in your wallet), receipts (transfer to files when you get home — see below), too many coins (unless it's a major part of the currency in your country) .

CLOTHES AND ACCESSORIES

Clothing is an area where our best-laid plans for order often go awry: our garments frequently end up slung over chairs, tossed on the bed, crumpled in piles on the floor, and spilling out of dresser drawers.

But by the same token, taking time to put away our clothes properly will go a very long way in keeping our bedrooms looking neat. Getting ready in a messy environment puts you in an out-of-sorts mood right from the get go, whereas waking up to a neat room in the morning really helps get your day started off on the right foot. Plus, proper care and storage of your clothes will make them last longer, saving you big money.

Dresser. There are a variety of ways to organize your dresser — you might choose to group clothes together by weight, season, or use. It also depends on how many drawers your particular dresser has. Here's how I do mine:

- Top drawer: underwear, socks, undershirts.

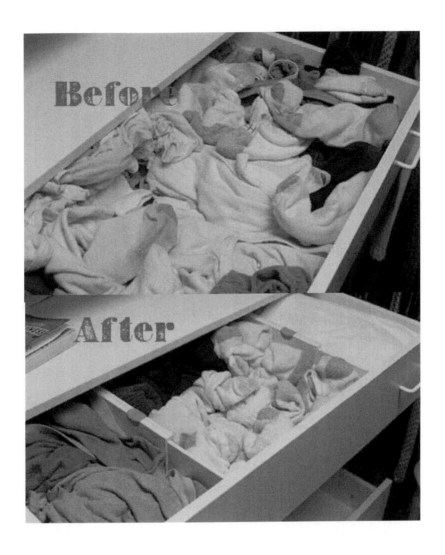

Drawer dividers are handy for keeping your underwear/sock drawer from becoming a chaotic mess and can help organize your others drawers as well. The expandable dividers seen here are quite handy, but a little pricey; if you're on a budget, shoe boxes or tissue boxes from which the top panel has been removed can also work.

- Second drawer: Fill it with the things you reach for most. Mine has got t-shirts and workout clothes.
- Third Drawer: Shorts, pants, sweaters. You might also put these types of items on a shelf in your closet.

I put my seasonal-specific clothes in a plastic tub depending on the season, and then rotate them into the dresser as the weather warms or cools.

More dresser tips:

- Even when you stack your clothes into nice piles inside your dresser drawers, as soon as you pull something out that's in the middle or bottom of the stack, the piles topple over into amish-mashed heap. A method that will keep things a bit neater is the file fold method. My drawers are too shallow for it, but it allows you to see all your garment choices and draw one out without disrupting things. You fold your t-shirts and place them in a drawer up and down like a file, instead of laying them horizontally. A YouTube search will show you specifically how to do it.

- Twice a year, take everything out of your drawers, remove anything you haven't worn in a year and donate those garments, then refold everything and put it back.

Closet rod. Some men do away with the dresser altogether, getting a little two-drawer container for socks and underwear and hanging everything else up. I'm personally kind of weirded out by t-shirts and jeans that are hung up, but to each their own. There are, however, some things that regardless of whether you have a dresser or not should be hung up, and hung up properly.

The following tips will help prolong the life of your clothes, and ensure they're ready to wear when you take them off the hanger:

- If your hang-able clothes are still clean when you take them off, put them right back on a hanger instead of leaving them crumpled up on the floor, which will create stubborn wrinkles. Hanging your worn garments will allow them to return to their natural shape.
- Check the garment for stains and offending scents before returning it to the hanger.
- Remove belts and heavy items in the pockets before placing the garment on the hanger, as they will stretch and distort it.
- Button the top and third button down on shirts to prevent wrinkles and the collar from spreading out on the hanger.
- After hanging up a suit or dress trousers you've worn that day, brush the garment gently with a clean, natural bristle brush. Doing this removes dirt and food that has accumulated on the outer layers before they have the chance to settle into the fabric. Regular brushing can double or even triple the time between which a garment will need to be taken to the cleaners.
- Never use wire hangers to hang any of your clothes. With too little surface area to properly support the garment, the wire will cut into the fabric and cause creases and damage.
- Use quality wood shirt hangers (at least ¼-inch thick) and wood suit hangers (at least 1-inch thick at the shoulders) to hang up your suits and nice shirts. Quality hangers are a little pricey, but certainly worth it when it comes to prolonging the life of a $400 suit.
- Don't put sweaters and knit shirts on a hanger, even a wide

one, as it will stretch them. Store sweaters and the like in your dresser or on a closet shelf.

• Don't crowd clothes together on the closet rod — maintain at least ½-inch between garments for airflow and ease of selection. This will give odors a chance to dissipate, and prevent the creasing, wrinkling, and fuzz transfer that can result from garments being smooshed together.

• Give clothes, especially nice items like suits, a day to rest in-between wearings when possible. This will give the fabric time to release its moisture, reshape, and rejuvenate.

• If clothing is going to be hung for more than a couple of months without being worn, consider placing it in a breathable garment bag to prevent dust accumulation.

Shoe organizer. Shoes tend to get left everywhere and end up all over the house or the closet floor. We've all had those frustrating times where we can find one shoe, but not the other, even when we're sure its mate must be close by! So get a shoe organizer — they come in a variety of styles from space-saving ones that hang from your closet bar, to racks that sit on the floor.

Here are a couple of additional shoe storage tips:

- When you remove leather shoes, slip a cedar shoe tree inside them. Shoe trees maintain the shape of the shoe, prevent the leather from warping in a way that would promote premature cracking, absorb excess moisture from the soles and leather, and prolong the life of the shoes.

- Give your shoes a 24-hour breather between wearings when possible to allow them to shed their moisture and rejuvenate.

Tie rack. Ties are often made from high quality, but fragile, materials like silk. So you want to take care of them in a way that prolongs their life. That care begins with getting a tie rack. The best way to store your ties is vertically, as the gravity will naturally smooth out their wrinkles.

More tie care tips:

- Store knit ties by rolling them up and placing them in a box or drawer. Hanging up a knit tie will stretch it out.
- Always untie your tie all the way when removing it. To save time, or because they fear they won't remember how to tie the same knot again, some men leave their ties tied, and just loosen the knot enough to slip it over their heads. The next day they slip the tie back on, and tighten it up. Don't do this. Leaving a tie tied will damage the fabric and shorten its lifespan over time.
- Instead of yanking off the tie and stretching the fabric, remove it using the same steps you tied it with, only now in reverse order. This method is the gentlest way to remove a tie.
- As with your other nice clothes, try to give ties a day of rest between wearings, to allow them to regain their natural shape.

Silent valet. Also known as a "clothes valet," or "valet stand," these fixtures were popular with the gentlemen of yesteryear. They're designed for the efficient man who wants his morning routine to be as smooth and stress-free as possible. Silent valets are set up to let you lay out your entire outfit for the next day the night before (and to hang up your clothes at the end of the day). They come with a place to hang your suit jacket, pants, shirt, and tie, along with a shelf for your shoes and a drawer for your pocket accoutrements. I've never tried one myself, but have had several readers email me about them over the years to sing their praises.

Document Box

As you set up a life on your own, you'll begin to accumulate a boat load of important documents like tax returns, college transcripts, car titles, rent leases, and credit reports. You'll likely encounter situations where you'll be required to cough-up these documents in order to file your taxes or to prove you've paid for something. You don't want to waste hours of your life searching every nook and cranny in your apartment for a stupid piece of paper simply because you didn't take the time to organize.

One habit I recommend starting right away is filing important paperwork in a document box (or file cabinet, if you have one). Your box doesn't have to be anything fancy. My first document box was just a cheap plastic container you can pick up at any office supply store for $10. Now I keep most of mine and Kate's important paperwork in a file drawer. I also recently acquired a safety deposit box where I plan on putting a few of my really important legal documents.

What sort of documents should you file away in your document box? There are seven broad categories of paperwork you should plan on keeping. Create a folder for each and start placing the suggested documents in them.

Society is at a crossroads where many documents can be digitized and found online, while some things still require a hard copy. If you can digitize something, do it. But when in doubt, retain a hard copy, too.

Identification
- Certified copy of your birth certificate. Your parents

probably have your original birth certificate on file. Before you leave home, get your own certified copy. You'll need it every now and then to prove your identification, like when you apply for a passport. You'll need to contact the vital records service of the state you were born in to get your copy.

- Social Security card
- Passport
- Photo copy of your driver's license

Insurance

Create a folder where you'll store all the documents relating to the various types of insurance you may have. One folder labeled "Insurance" should be enough when you're first starting out. As you acquire more types of insurance, you can get more granular with your foldering. Your folder should have copies of:

- Car insurance policy
- Health insurance policy
- Renter's or home insurance
- Life insurance policy
- Disability insurance policy

School

When you're applying for graduate programs or jobs, you'll likely need copies of your transcripts and diplomas. Store those in a folder labeled "School."

Medical

- Immunization record

- List of allergies
- Names and numbers of doctors. When you visit a new doctor, they'll likely call your previous doctor to get your medical records. It's nice to have those numbers handy.
- Eyeglass/contacts prescription

Legal

While you might not have too many legal documents when you're first starting out in life, it's a good idea to create a folder for the ones you'll likely collect throughout adulthood.

- Rental leases
- Power of attorney
- Advanced directive (living will)
- Will (when you get one)
- Marriage license (when you get hitched)
- Any other contracts you enter into

Financial

Place all your financial related documents in this folder. These include:

- Bank statements for your checking and savings account
- Info about your retirement savings
- Info about your loans

Warranties/Receipts/Owner's Manuals

I like to have a folder where I stash all the documents for all my big purchases. Whenever one of my appliances goes kaput, I know exactly where to find the owner's manual and receipt. Much better than searching random kitchen drawers for those things. Of course, many manuals can be found online these days, so you can go that route, although it's still nice to have something you can easily crouch down with in the basement or something.

It's also a good idea to digitize receipts. That way if you're out and about, you can access them anywhere, anytime on your phone.

Taxes

When you're done filing your taxes, you need to hold onto a copy of your return and the accompanying paperwork for a few years because, 1) you might get audited by the IRS, and 2) you never know when you'll need to report your previous year's income for a rental agreement or loan.

Create a folder for each year's taxes. I always start mine January 1st. That's when I begin collecting all the paperwork so I can file by April 15. After I've shipped everything off to the IRS, I place my folder that contains the copy of the return along with other documents in my file drawer.

How long should you keep old tax files? It depends. If you're a salaried employee working for someone else, three years should be sufficient. The IRS can audit these types of filers for any reason within a three-year period. If you own a business or your taxes are more complex, hold onto your files for at least six years.

Tools and Emergency Supplies

You should also have a dedicated place where you keep all of your tools and emergency supplies — these are things you definitely don't want to be running around hunting for when you need them!

Do It Now!

So you're committed to adopting "a place for everything and everything in its place" as a maxim in your life, and you've established the best places to put your things. How do you now develop the habit of actually putting your things in those places?

By Living the Principle of Do It Now!

Without constant, small exertions of effort, your life will always tend towards chaos. Always doing the little things that need to get done right away will prevent them from piling up into a giant, overwhelming mess that can get your life off track, or, at the least, add unnecessary stress to it.

As soon as you're finished using something, put it away. As soon as something you need to do crosses your mind, take care of it immediately. When you open a cabinet to get something, close it. When you run out of TP, put another roll on the holder. When you take off your clothes, put them in the hamper. When you drop something on the floor, pick it up. By living the principle of Do It Now, you can easily keep your house and life in order and live with a manly sense of peace and confidence.

To illustrate the Do It Now principle, we had actor and

filmmaker Jordan Crowder produce an awesome video in the style of the 1950s instructional films we've included in a couple of the posts in this series. It's a great video that perfectly sums up the principle, so take a gander by visiting: *http://youtu.be/auXMHMAZL6Y*.

CONCLUSION

You've made it to the end of our 31-day boot camp on becoming a well-adjusted adult. Congratulations! Just by going through these exercises, you've put yourself leaps and bounds ahead of many of your peers.

While we couldn't have possibly covered every single skill a young man needs to successfully live on his own in just one book, I really believe we hit nearly all of the important essentials. If you're a man who's been living on his own for a long time now, I hope the book provided an interesting and helpful refresher, and maybe even imparted some newly-learned tips, on skills that we truly use our whole lives through (and all need reminders on from time to time). If you're a young man heading out on his own right now, our sincere wish is that this book has given you a sense of direction, competence, and confidence about this new and exciting season in your life. Make sure to visit *artofmanliness.com* for more tips on becoming a thriving adult and mastering the art of manliness.

You now have an important cache of information at your disposal, and knowing, as GI Joe has taught us, is half the battle. The other half will be won by honing your skills in the only way they can be: through practical experience and much trial and error. Don't be afraid to make mistakes — just commit yourself to always learning from them. We wish you the very best as you embark on whatever new adventure awaits you; wherever it leads, we hope you enjoy the ride!

ACKNOWLEDGEMENT

This was our first time self-publishing a book and without the help and hard work of several amazing people, we wouldn't have been able to do this. Kate and I would be remiss if we didn't thank them publicly.

First, to Jeremy Anderberg, without which this book would not exist. Thank you for initially editing the articles for the series during our insane, non-stop August. Thank you for then editing this book over and over again, making sure things were just right with an unwavering patience and steely perseverance. Where others might have gone nuts or given up, you kept on polishing. We couldn't have done this without you!

To Ted Slampyak, for his amazing illustrations that are peppered throughout the book and that grace the cover. You're always a pleasure to work with.

To Eric and Hannah Granata and the folks at Screen Four Solutions. They took care of making the book available in multiple digital formats as well as lining things up so we could offer a paperback version. They did all this while simultaneously working on other big projects for us, kicking butt at a full-time job, and taking care of house full of kiddos. The Granatas know how to hustle and we're glad we know them.

To Antonio Centeno. First, for your contributions to the book, but also for your years of friendship and partnership. You're truly a class act. It's been fun watching your own business grow and evolve and we wish you all the success in the world and look forward to our future friendship and partnership.

To Darren Bush for showing us how to fix a running toilet as well as his regular outdoorsy contributions to the site. AoM would be a lot less manly without you, sir.

To Matt Moore for his contributions on cooking and for his monthly contributions to the site. Congratulations on all the success and we wish you all the best on your second book.

To Erikka Hedberg. We just met you, but we're glad we did. Thanks for cranking out the paperback formatting so fast and doing such a great job with it. We look forward to working with you again in the future.

ABOUT THE AUTHORS

Brett and Kate McKay are the founders and owners of The Art of Manliness (*artofmanliness.com*), the largest independent men's lifestyle site on the web. As of this publishing (2013), the Art of Manliness receives over 14 million page views a month and has over 170,000 daily subscribers.

6011699R00242

Printed in Great Britain
by Amazon.co.uk, Ltd.,
Marston Gate.